RAILWAYS OF THE BLACK COUNTRY

VOLUME ONE: THE BYWAYS

NED WILLIAMS

1 : (frontispiece) Level Street, Brierley Hill. A Barclay 0-4-05T and tipping-wagon of slag represents the industrial face of the Black Country. Behind the smoke the rolling countryside beneath Netherton Church is not quite the rural enclave it seems as many pits, and more recently open cast mining, have all contributed to a landscape that has now been turned into an "Enterprise Zone"! *(2nd May 1959, P.J. Shoesmith)*

ISBN 0 9500533 8 4

URALIA PRESS
1984

Uralia Press: 23 Westland Road, Wolverhampton, West Midlands, WV3 9NZ.

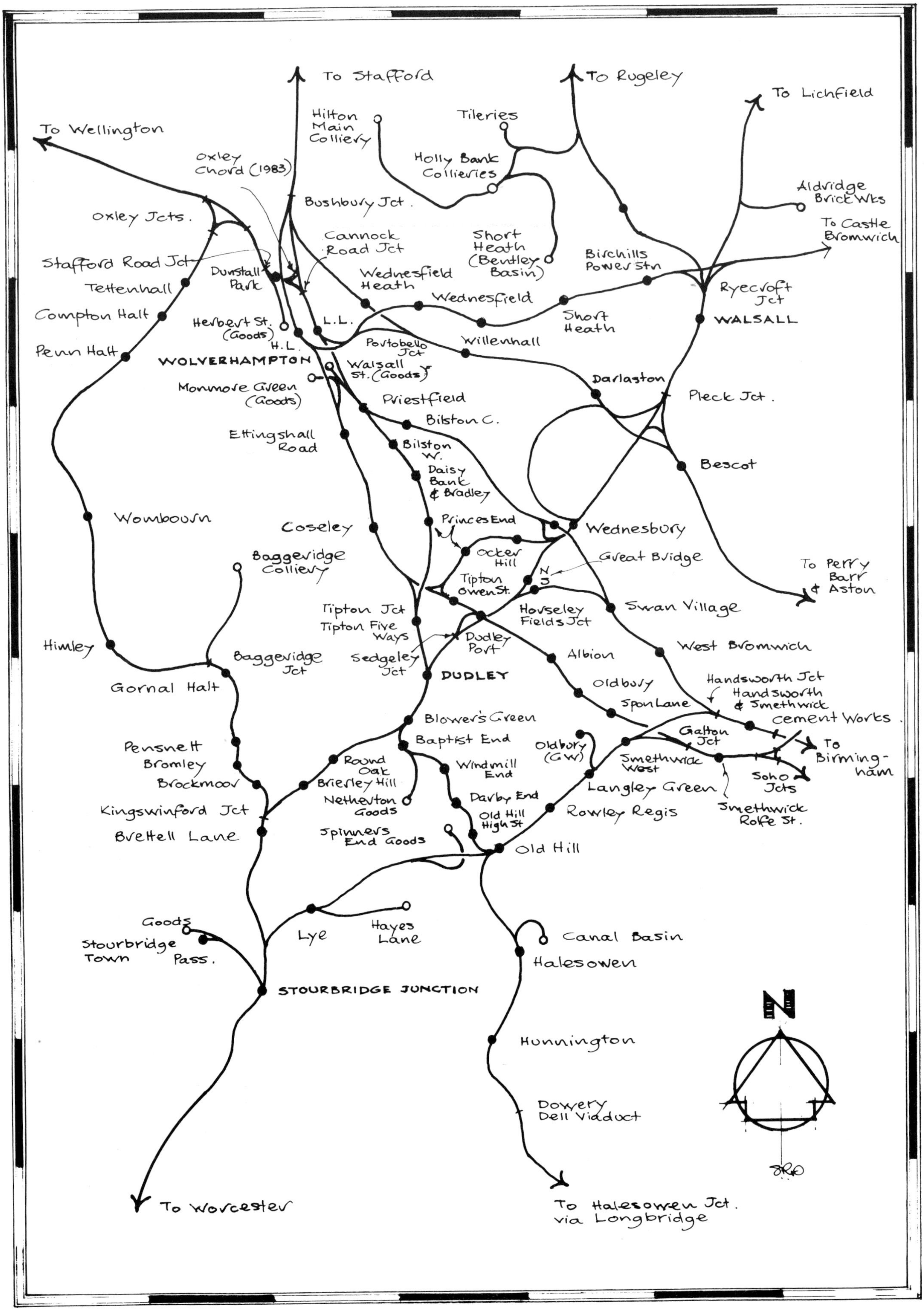
To Stafford
To Rugeley
To Lichfield
To Wellington
Hilton Main Colliery
Tileries
Holly Bank Collieries
Oxley Chord (1983)
Bushbury Jct.
Aldridge Brick Wks
To Castle Bromwich
Oxley Jcts.
Cannock Road Jct
Short Heath (Bentley Basin)
Birchills Power Stn
Stafford Road Jct
Dunstall Park
Wednesfield Heath
Wednesfield
Ryecroft Jct
Tettenhall
Compton Halt
Herbert St. (Goods)
L.L.
Short Heath
WALSALL
H.L.
Portobello Jct
Willenhall
Penn Halt
WOLVERHAMPTON
Walsall St. (Goods)
Monmore Green (Goods)
Darlaston
Priestfield
Pleck Jct.
Bilston C.
Ettingshall Road
Bilston W.
Bescot
Daisy Bank & Bradley
Wombourn
Princes End
Coseley
Wednesbury
Ocker Hill
Baggeridge Colliery
Great Bridge
To Perry Barr & Aston
N
S
Tipton Owen St.
Tipton Jct
Horseley Fields Jct
Swan Village
Tipton Five Ways
Dudley Port
Himley
Baggeridge Jct
Sedgeley Jct
Albion
West Bromwich
DUDLEY
Gornal Halt
Oldbury
Handsworth Jct
Handsworth & Smethwick
Spon Lane
Cement Works
Blower's Green
Galton Jct
To Birmingham
Pensnett
Baptist End
Oldbury (GW)
Bromley
Round Oak
Brierley Hill
Windmill End
Smethwick West
Soho Jcts
Brockmoor
Langley Green
Netherton Goods
Darby End
Kingswinford Jct
Rowley Regis
Smethwick Rolfe St.
Old Hill High St
Brettell Lane
Spinners End Goods
Old Hill
Goods
Lye
Hayes Lane
Canal Basin
Stourbridge Town
Pass.
Halesowen
STOURBRIDGE JUNCTION
N
Hunnington
Dowery Dell Viaduct
To Worcester
To Halesowen Jct. via Longbridge

There is something exciting about photographing railways. Trains, and the weather, are usually unpredictable despite the sciences of timetabling and meteorology and if the photographer is concerned with all the other components of his picture the problems of composition are enormous. A clearly visible train in the right place is only one of the criteria used in selecting these photos, what really matters is the "sense of location": an evocation of railways in the Black Country.

The Black Country is an industrial area, formerly in the south of the county of Staffordshire and the northern fringe of Worcestershire, where an unusually thick seam of coal approached the surface, and iron and limestone could once be found. The railways did not create the original industrialisation of this area. The canals did that. However from the middle of the nineteenth century onwards railways crossed the area, linked it with far-off places, and created a complex local network of lines. This book does not set out to provide a new definitive history of these lines. It is a picture book – trying to place on record what the landscape looked like when railways formed a part of it, criss-crossing canals, serving mines and factories, weaving between spoil heaps, whistling through the many small communities, villages and towns of the area.

In recent times a number of books of railway photographs have appeared to deal with the "West Midlands" but most of them give scant attention to the Black Country. A pioneer in trying to put matters right was Michael Hale but his books are almost exclusively about railways in the age of steam and rely exclusively on his own photographic work. However striking and informative his pictures are I have felt the need to bring together the work of many other photographers to really cover the subject comprehensively, and I feel it is wrong to imagine that local railways ceased to be interesting somewhere in the middle 1960s!

Both the railways and the landscape through which they pass are continually undergoing change. It is this dynamic quality that makes recording the changes so interesting. The changes take place in a context that we call "the legacy of the past". Thus, as steam disappeared in the mid sixties, and the railways contracted, the Black Country landscape included many nineteenth century features as well as components from the first five decades of this century. The seventies and early eighties have seen much of this heritage destroyed, an emerging consciousness of a need to preserve some things, and the dawn of a new High–Tec Industrial Revolution that shows no interest in coal or iron and steel and the traditional engineering skills of the Blackcountryman. The spoil heaps are turned into parks, new housing obliterates the past. Cooling towers, church spires and factory chimneys are wiped off the horizon, town centres are transformed, but possibly the changes that took place in the past were just as dramatic.

For the railway photographer the task of portraying railways in their setting has become more difficult. Signals and signal boxes, lineside and station buildings, bridges and crossings, sidings and people at work: all these are the details that once brought railway photographs to life, so look carefully at the more recent pictures in this book and consider how photographers are meeting the challenge.

It will be obvious that the photographs in this selection have been chosen for what they show, rather than as masterpieces of photography as an art. I hope it is equally obvious from what I have said that taking a really informative photograph is no easy matter. Therefore I feel very privileged to have been able to survey the collections of the photographers who have contributed to the book, and also thankful that such people did venture into this "Cinderella" area.

This volume sets out to portray the railway *"byways"* of the Black Country. I realise that the term *"byway"* will create a great deal of argument. For example, many readers will not regard the West Midland line as one, but I feel it certainly became one by the 1960s. Even the GWR main line became a byway after 1967 and today two small stretches of it, to Moxley and to Handsworth, certainly deserve that designation. In Volume Two, the GWR main line can appear in its former glory, plus the LMS "Stour Valley" line, the "Grand Junction" line, and the "Stourbridge Extension" line. (Can anyone help find photographs of the byways that once joined the latter, e.g. the Spinners End and Hayes Branches?). Volume Two can also bring together photographs of the main railway centres of the Black Country: Walsall, Wolverhampton, Stourbridge Junction, and Dudley. If anyone has photographs of these places, the main lines, the sheds at Ryecroft, Bescot, Stafford Road, Oxley and Stourbridge, or any of the byways that have been missed, I would be delighted to hear from them.

Finally, I would like to point out that I have tried to bring together previously – unpublished photographs. I draw your attention, therefore, to the bibliography and to the pictures by Michael Hale, Michael Mensing, John Dew, and Peter Shoesmith, that have already appeared in print. "By Rail to Wombourn" and "By Rail to Halesowen" are both unfortunately out-of-print but the photographs of those lines included in this book are chosen to complement the illustrations in those two books.

And when you have looked at all the pictures, grab your camera and set out to explore the railways of the Black Country.

Ned Williams
July 1984

Acknowledgements

A book of this kind is a compilation of material produced by many people. I am grateful for the generous contribution of photographs, expert knowledge, and time, from the following people:

Vivian Morgan
P.J. Shoesmith
Roger Carpenter
Ray Shill
Mike Wood
Norman Glover
John Dew
Jack Haddock
Robert Selvey
Michael Mensing
Martin Shenton
Geoff Bannister
John James
Edgar Rumble
Jim Garbett
Ron Smallshire
Simon Dewey
Jim Evans
Paul Dorney
Richard Taylor
Ted Higgs
Keith Hodgkins
Roger Monk
W.A. Camwell
John L. Smith
Philip Barnard
Vic Smallshire
Bert Pritchard
Lionel J. Lee
John Harris
Brian Robbins
Roger Crombleholme

Dudley Libraries, Birmingham Libraries.
Dave Whyley (Black Country Society Collection)
Industrial Railway Society (Ken Cooper Collection).
John Van Leerzum (Phil Lycett Collection).
Real Photographs

– and in production of the book:

John Revill (Design)
Chris Wigg (Text)
Mauline Watson (Planning)
Jan Endean (Photo-processing).

The line from Priestfield, just outside Wolverhampton, to Stourbridge Junction, would not be considered a "by-way" by many people who remember GWR trains to Paddington traversing the route but the fact that the section north of Dudley has now disappeared and that south Dudley it sees only sparse freight traffic suggests that is was not really a major part of the national network.

The line was built as the northern section of the Oxford Worcester and Wolverhampton Railway, involving many financial and legal problems. The OWWR ran from just north of Oxford to a junction with the Grand Junction Railway just north of Wolverhampton, entering the Black Country near Stourbridge and crossing the central ridge that bisects the region at Dudley in a tunnel. The line was opened from Droitwich to Stourbridge in May 1852 and to Dudley by the end of that year. Wolverhampton Low Level was reached in 1854, and a goods station in Wolverhampton, at Walsall Street, opened the following year.

The OWWR (The "Old, Worse & Worse") became part of the West Midland Railway in 1860, and, in turn, this became part of the GWR in 1863, thereafter being known as the "West Midland" line of that company. The local service between Wolverhampton and Stourbridge Junction provided its passengers with the perfect transect of the Black Country and served communities that worked in a real cross-section of the industries that defined it.

This passenger service was withdrawn on 30th July 1962 and at the beginning of the following year the goods-only line became part of the London Midland Region of BR, confusing the loyalties of many railwaymen. Dudley Station lost its remaining passenger services in 1964 and the site was cleared to make way for a new Freight Liner Terminal in 1967. The section of the West Midlands north of Dudley closed the following year. The remaining section of the West Midlands from Dudley to Stourbridge Junction shares its precarious existence as a by-way with the South Staffordshire line that links it to Bescot.

2 : It is difficult to pick one location that provides the perfect picture of the Black Country's railway byways at work. Perhaps the areas around and between Great Bridge and Wednesbury provide the right ingredients but I have seen few photographs that have exploited them satisfactorily. Perhaps the areas around and between Blowers Green and Round Oak, on the other side of the ridge, are equally as good. This view of Parkhead Viaduct has many of the right ingredients, an interesting railway structure, a canal, distant steelworks, rooftops, chimneys, trees and a far-off hint of the Clent Hills. GW Manor class 4-6-0, 7806, *"Cockington Manor"*, brings a pigeon train back from Malvern to Wolverhampton on 19th May 1964. Twenty years later BR have ceased carrying pigeon traffic, the distant steelworks have closed but the canal has been revived and the occasional train still crosses the viaduct. *(Richard Taylor)*

3 : A GW class 51xx 2-6-2T, 4173, approaches Priestfield Station, on 28th April 1962, on a local train to Wolverhampton. The main line from Birmingham Snow Hill can be clearly seen curving into Priestfield on the left. The West Midland proceeds straight ahead as befits the company that arrived first. It is not absolutely certain that the station existed when the OWWR trains started running on 1st July 1854, or even when the GWR trains joined them four months later. There is evidence that the station opened on 2nd July 1855. The little building on the left was originally used by a Railway Clearing House "checker", recording the volume of traffic passing on each line. Although all the tracks have now disappeared the platforms have survived into the eighties. (Note: 4173 later hauled the last train from Wolverhampton to Stourbridge). *(John Dew)*

4 : A GW class 57xx 0-6-0PT, 3677, pauses at Bilston West, the first intermediate station south of Priestfield, and one of three stations that once claimed to serve Bilston. Close to Bilston West the GWR had its connection to the internal railway system of Bilston Steelworks. (28th April 1962). *(John Dew)*

5 : South of Bilston the West Midland line passed Daisy Bank and Bradley, attractively located in a cutting, and headed for Princes End and Coseley. A relatively modern concrete bridge can be seen linking the booking office to the two platforms. GW "Manor" class, 7816, *"Frilsham Manor"* can be seen heading south on the 1 p.m. Wolverhampton-Stourbridge Jct. train on 2nd December 1961. *(John Dew)*

6 : Princes End and Coseley Signal Box was just south of the station and once controlled a busy little yard. A down loop that passed behind the box, on which some carriages are stabled, also once provided access to a siding serving a wagon-repair depot. *(Paul Dorney)*

The West Midland Line

7 : GW class 57xx 0-6-0PT, 9624, pauses at Dudley on an Up West Midland line local train on 25th November 1961. Note that the buildings on the GWR side of the station seemed a little more substantial than those on the LMS, on the right. All the buildings were demolished in 1967 when the site was cleared to make way for the Freightliner Terminal. *(John Dew)*

8 : The site of Dudley station in 1984: Class 58, 58002, pulls class 86, 86245, from the Up line onto the down line and thence into the Freightliner Terminal on the morning of 8th May 1984, as a linesman descends from the signal box. An hour or two later 86245 was named *"Dudley Castle"* by the Earl of Dudley, and was then towed back to Bescot. After the last passenger train had run in 1964, Dudley remained open for parcels traffic, later handled in the LMS goods shed. The station was demolished during the winter of 66/67 and work began on the Freightliner Terminal. The new signal box, on the left of the picture, came into use in July 1967 and the new terminal opened on 6th November 1967. Perhaps such a place cannot be considered a "byway" but its use has declined and it has been threatened with closure since 1981. *(Ned Williams)*

9 : A GW class 51xx 2-6-2T, 4173, pauses at the remains of Blowers Green Station on 28th April 1962. It has just brought its local train through the tunnel from Dudley and has crossed into the south-western half of the Black Country. The OWWR opened a station called Netherton, just south of this point, when the line reached Dudley towards the end of 1852. When the line to Old Hill (The Bumble Hole line) opened on 1st March 1878 this station was built between the tunnel and the junction, and was called Dudley Southside and Netherton. It was renamed "Blowers Green" in August 1921. It closed, along with the other West Midland line stations in 1962, despite the irony that the Dudley-Old Hill trains continued to pass through without stopping for another two years. *(John Dew)*

10 : GW Hall class, 6927, *"Lilford Hall"* passes Blowers Green Junction, just south of the station with the Tavistock-Crewe freight on 10th August 1965. The line to Old Hill curves away sharply to the left and sidings occupy the site of the original OWWR "Netherton" station. In the distance are the factories of the Cinder Bank area, including Messrs. Grazebrook's works which were the home of engine seen in picture number 198. The siding on the extreme left of the fan of sidings seen beyond the signal box provided access to Grazebrook's system. Twenty years ago Blowers Green was still a busy place but today all signs of the branch and sidings have disappeared. *(Richard Taylor)*

11 : The West Midland line passed under Cinder Bank, from which this picture was taken and on the up side stood Blowers Green Sidings Signal Box – of which no trace remains. Sidings in the Blowers Green area once served Metallisation, S.G.B., and Messrs. Goodyear, as well as Grazebrook's. Through all this industrial activity ran the picturesquely named *"Pear Tree Lane"*, seen just behind the signal box. The picture was taken on 2nd April 1965. *(Richard Taylor)*

12 : GW 56xx class 0-6-2T, No. 5659, brings a pick-up goods across Parkhead Viaduct on 23rd April 1963. A number of canals, or canal arms, converge at this point, and on the far side of the viaduct they make for the Dudley Canal Tunnel. The Trust formed to preserve the canal tunnel and the British Waterways Board have transformed the area, culminating in the re-opening of the tunnel in 1972. On the far side of the viaduct the track curves away past Round Oak North Signal Box and into another area of great industrial fascination and complexity. *(Richard Taylor)*

A short distance from Parkhead Viaduct the line encountered more industrial activity. Behind the Dudley Drop Forging Co. stood Round Oak North Signal Box (later replaced with a lever frame). The Woodside Branch, a mere half a mile in length, on the up side, served Hill and Smith, Southern's timber yard, a tip belonging to the Austin Motor Co., Messrs. Cochrane's, and a slag tip for Round Oak Steelworks. (The Earl of Dudley's engines travelled over GWR metals to this siding from Round Oak South). Just north of Round Oak South Box, the Pensnett Railway crossed the West Midland line on the level. (See picture 166).

13 : GW 56xx class, 6678, 0-6-2T, approaches the level crossing with an up goods in the early sixties. There is no truth in the legend that the Earl of Dudley's trains had priority on this crossing, despite the fact the Pensnett Railway occupied the site first. The crossing was not finally removed until November 1983. *(Viv Morgan)*

14 : Round Oak South Box, finally taken out of use when the crossing was removed, witnesses the passing of LMS "Jubilee" class 4-6-0, 5690, *"Leander"*, restored to LMS livery and number by preservationists, on 4th December 1981. *(Edgar Rumble)*

15 : Round Oak South Signal Box can just be seen through the arch of the bridge that carries the main Dudley-Brierley Hill road over the West Midland line. GW class 57xx 0-6-0PT, 4696, draws into the up platform of Round Oak station on 28th April 1962. *(John Dew)*

16 : A GW "Manor" class 4-6-0, 7806, *"Cockington Manor"* pulls into the up platform at Brierley Hill beneath a footbridge that seems rather scrappy compared with those at Bilston West and Daisy Bank, but more elegant than the concrete structure at Princes End. It seems that the original OWWR station was at Round Oak, and that this "Brierley Hill" station was opened on 1st December 1858, the footbridge being added twenty years later.The station had no yard of its own due to the proximity of

Moor Lane Yard but there was a siding on the up side that handled traffic from Messrs. Marsh and Baxter. Brierley Hill remained open to handle parcels traffic, after passenger trains were withdrawn, until January 1967, and the site was cleared in 1968. (Picture taken 21st January 1961). *(John Dew)*

17 : Just before running under Moor Lane Bridge the line passed Kingswinford Junction North Signal Box on the up side. The extensive sidings and the junction with the Kingswinford Branch were always more under the control of the South Box, which is still in use today. This 1968 view of the North Box was taken shortly before its demolition. *(Paul Dorney)*

18 : From Moor Lane Bridge this excellent view of the northern end of Moor Lane Yard was obtained on 8th May 1957. A GW 28xx class 2-8-0 , 2817, is passing the yard on a down goods. In 1984 Messrs. Stevens & Williams Glassworks still dominate the view, much of the signalling has disappeared and the sidings have been remodelled to form Brierley Hill Steel Terminal, opened on 31st May 1965. *(John Dew)*

19 : Kingswinford Junction South Box and environs in 1966. GW 57xx class 0-6-0PT, 9608, is passing the signal box with an up train while two "panniers" are waiting to double-head a train from Pensnett off the branch. *(Paul Dorney)*

20 : Kingswinford Junction: 10th May 1984. BR class 45 1-Co-Co-1, 45012, returns to the Steel Terminal Yard from Stourbridge Junction. Note: a) to the left of the engine the yard headshunt has been singled (once upon a time a GWR water tank serviced engines on these sidings), b) The Kingswinford Branch has been singled, and c) the Up sidings that once served the pens and wharf of Messrs. Marsh & Baxter have almost completely been removed. Once ten trains could pass this box in one hour, today barely ten trains pass in a whole day. *(Ned Williams)*

21 : Leaving Kingswinford Junction the West Midland line traversed an area associated with brickworks, and, more recently, open-cast mining. A GW class 51xx 2-6-2T runs bunker first into Brettell Lane station on a local stopping train on 21st January 1961. *(John Dew)*

22 : By 1968, when this picture was taken, the building on the down platform at Brettell Lane was in a sorry state, name boards had disappeared and tracks into the down-side yard had been lifted. The OWWR was not a prosperous concern and many of its station buildings were of simple wooden construction so it is tempting to wonder if this building dated from the 1840s. (The GWR did later improve the stations, build footbridges, etc.) It is also tempting to wonder if passengers ever alighted here between 1925 and 1932 to catch the railmotor on the Wombourn branch? *(Ned Williams)*

23 : The yard on the up side of Brettell Lane, again photographed in 1968, once featured a reasonably large goods shed. On the extreme right the girders of the bridge carrying the running lines across the Stourbridge canal can be seen. In the background the spoil heaps of open-cast mining dominate the scene. (The Western Boundary Fault threw coal and fire-clay close to the surface in this area). *(Roger Crombleholme)*

24 : An unusual photograph taken in the down side yard in the late 1950s shows not only the Matisa plate-layer's vehicle but also sidings containing private-owner wagons, and, in the background, the splendid offices of Messrs. Harris & Pearson, manufacturers of refactory bricks. *(Phil Lycett)*

25 : In June 1972 the West Midland line was "diverted" in order that coal could be mined at a huge open cast pit between Brettell Lane and Amblecote. While the diversion lasted trains described a horse-shoe around the workings and when the mining finished a new straighter-than-before embankment was constructed to carry the line across the area. With the diversion in the foreground track-laying can be seen in this picture on the present course of the line. BR class 25, 25262, then numbered 7612 is in charge of the track-laying vehicle. *(John James)*

26 : On 6th September 1965 GW class 57xx 0-6-0PT, 3788, should have brought its train from Oxley to a halt at Moor Lane Yard, just north of Kingswinford Junction. The train ran away and finally came to rest below the Stambermill Viaduct, which carries the West Midland line across the valley of the Stour. *(John Dew)*

27 & 28 : LMS class 8F 2-8-0, 48651, attended the recovery of the wreck on 12th September 1965. The views obtained also show the position of the original timber viaduct, adjacent to its brick replacement built in the 1880s. *(27 : Edgar Rumble, 28 : Paul Dorney)*

29 : Having been temporarily stabled at Stourbridge Shed, GW 2251 class 0-6-0, 3205, passes Stourbridge North Junction on its way to the Severn Valley Railway on 25th March 1967. 3205 was the first steam locomotive to arrive on the SVR's preserved line and this was an historic event. From this book's point of view it is the only picture located so far which shows the signal box at the junction. (Almost entirely hidden behind 3205's tender!). Anyone working this box would have regarded the "Stourbridge Extension" line, heading for Birmingham in the foreground, as the branch and the West Midland as very much the "mainline". The box closed at the end of July 1978, and was demolished. *(John Dew)*

30 : The same location today – devoid of semaphore signals and signal box has only the girder of the bridge over Junction Road to prove that it is the same place. Frequent trains on the Stourbridge Extension line in the foreground contrast with the rarity of trains reaching the southern end of the West Midland line. On 11th June 1984 BR class 45 1-Co-Co-1 diesel, 45056, approaches Stourbridge Junction at about 7.50 a.m. with V66, the Bescot-Severn Tunnel Junction freight, consisting of only three wagons. *(Ned Williams)*

The Stourbridge Town Branch

Stourbridge Station opened by the OWWR on 1st May 1852 was just to the north of the present day Stourbridge Junction station, by Junction Road, then called Station Road. This was not very close to the centre of the town for passengers, and remote from the industries down in the Stour Valley for goods traffic. The West Midland line crept northwards across the Stour Valley on a wooden Stambermill Viaduct later the same year, and by the end of the decade a goods-only branch had been laid from the Amblecote side of the viaduct down to canal basin, across the High Street and into the works of John Bradley & Co. It seems that this line opened on 30th July 1859. The steep gradient descended by the line made it unsuitable for passenger traffic.

In 1874 the GWR obtained authority to build a new branch to Stourbridge Town. The new line left Stourbridge (Junction) at the southern end of the station and curved round very sharply to head for the town centre to a station at Foster Street. Beyond Foster Street the double track continued, for conveyance of goods traffic, down quite a spectacular gradient to the canal. A new goods station and canal transhipment facilities were being provided at Mill Meadow.

Passenger services on the branch commenced on 1st October 1879 and goods traffic began on 1st January 1880. (The original goods branch seems to have "faded away"). Further changes to the branch added to the complexity of its history.

In 1901 a new Stourbridge Junction station was opened, to the south of the original station, and the branch could now swing into the down side of this station at its northern end, thus assuming its present alignment. The passenger service was suspended altogether during the First World War, and later, in 1935, a signal box at the Town was closed and the branch worked as two parallel single tracks: one for passenger trains, the other for goods. (The former usually blocked at Foster Street by a wagon).

The goods yard was closed in 1965 and the goods line was subsequently lifted. Even the passenger service was threatened, but fortunately it still survives. The rather elegant station building has been demolished in order to extend the adjacent bus terminus and the single diesel railcar now stops at a short platform, sporting a bus shelter, just north of the original terminus. The frequency with which the train buzzes back and forth between Junction and Town must be some kind of record.

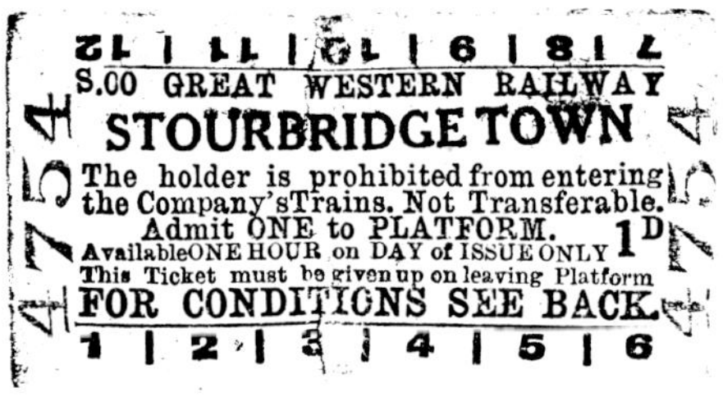
S.00 GREAT WESTERN RAILWAY
STOURBRIDGE TOWN
The holder is prohibited from entering the Company's Trains. Not Transferable.
Admit ONE to PLATFORM. 1D
Available ONE HOUR on DAY of ISSUE ONLY
This Ticket must be given up on leaving Platform
FOR CONDITIONS SEE BACK.
1 | 2 | 3 | 4 | 5 | 6

31 : GW class 14xx, 0-4-2T, 1414, waits in the Branch platform at Stourbridge Junction with its push-pull train for the Town on 10th September 1955 – a typical GW branch line scene usually associated with rural England rather than a major conurbation.
(P.J. Shoesmith)

32 : GW class 64xx, 0-6-0PT, 6424, leaves Stourbridge Junction with *"Wren"*, complete with wooden destination board next to the door. Meanwhile a goods train is waiting to come off the branch, behind 9782, on 2nd November 1963. *(John Dew)*

33 : Even today the Stourbridge Town Branch does play host to the occasional unusual train – but photographers usually find out about it too late. However, on 16th October 1955, GW class 74xx 0-6-0PT, 7429, was caught between the Junction and the Town with a special train for Chipperfield's Circus.
(John Dew)

34 : The changing scene at Stourbridge Town: A GW class 14xx 0-4-2T, 1414, is about to propel a wooden bodied GW push-pull unit back to the junction as a Midland Red D5B stands outside the station. Note that both tracks were still in situ beyond the station, when this picture was taken on 9th September 1957. *(John Dew)*

35 : GW "streamlined" railcar W14W stands at Stourbridge Town on 12th August 1957. Note: only the goods-line is clearly visible beyond the station in this picture. *(John Dew)*

36 : 0-6-0PT, 6434, propels *"Wren"* out of Stourbridge Town on 2nd November 1963. In this picture the station fencing has been renewed and the original wooden nameboard, with its white letters on a black background, has been replaced with a new enamel sign in Western Region colours. An "iron-mink" wagon body has also appeared on the platform and the passenger-carrying track now stops at a buffer stop and wall. Stourbridge's Odeon, seen behind the station building, has put up some new neon lettering, but was doomed to close 16th June 1973. *(John Dew)*

37 & 38 : British Rail have continued the GWR tradition of working some branch-line services with single diesel railcars. In pictures 37 and 38, both taken in 1967, a green-liveried railcar stands alongside the disused goods track. In picture 37 it can be seen that this was truncated at Foster Street before being lifted completely. In picture 38 the view from the buffer stops shows the Vauxhall Road footbridge, from which so many photographs of the station were taken. This bridge has now been demolished.

(John Dew)

39 : The branch has been reduced to a single track supporting a BR class 122 blue-liveried single diesel railcar, but this late 70s view was not quite to survive intact into the 80s. In 1979, its centenary year, the building was demolished and the station moved a few yards northwards. Today's railcar (in blue and grey) halts alongside a bus shelter and portacabin! The modern station name boards (black on white) have reverted to the GWR practice of simply calling the station "Stourbridge".

(Roger Crombleholme)

40 : GW class 57xx 0-6-0PT (with original-style cab) 5754, climbs towards Stourbridge Town from the goods yard in June 1955. The bridge and width of the formation clearly reflect the original provision of double track on this section. In the background can be seen the long footbridge that crossed the throat of the yard, the gas works (served by their own sidings until the early 60s), and, on the skyline the right-hand side, the roof of Stourbridge Engine Shed. Modern housing has obliterated the open hillside on the right. *(John Dew)*

41 : Another GW class 57xx 0-6-0PT, with later style cab, works hard on the 1 in 27 gradient out of the Stour Valley from the goods yard, on 8th April 1961. The operating appendix declared, "In all cases guards working up or down branch trains must ride outside their van compartment at the hand brake in readiness to give instant attention." *(John Dew)*

42 : A view from the footbridge into Stourbridge Basin Goods Yard as a 57xx 0-6-0PT, 3729, starts the ascent with a train of empty wagons on 2nd November 1957. The yard, water tower, and substantial goods shed can all be seen clearly. Beyond the shed the tracks continued across Lower High Street to serve John Bradley & Co. The rails in the level crossing bore 3 feet 6 inches gauge grooves where the Dudley and Stourbridge Electric Tramways crossed them! The foundry at John Bradley & Co. was established by his half brother, James Foster. The latter, in partnership with Mr. Rastrick, expanded the business and *"Agenoria"* and the *"Stourbridge Lion"* were built there. *(John Dew)*

The Kingswinford Branch was built by the OWWR, and opened from Kingswinford Junction to Bromley Basin, on the Stourbridge Extension Canal, on 14th November 1858. The canal, purchased by the OWWR in 1847, brought traffic down from the Shut End area to the rail head at Bromley, but the branch itself was gradually extended northwards reaching Oak Farm colliery, just north of Shut End, by 1860. (The Pensnett Railway was extended into this area at the same time, joining the original Shut End Railway in 1865).

It would have remained a minor GWR goods branch but for plans to drag it into the company's scheme to link Wolverhampton and Bridgnorth! After several changes of plan this led to the upgrading of the Kingswinford Branch, as a double track line capable of carrying a passenger service as far as Baggeridge Junction, from which it continued as a single track line through Wombourn to Oxley, just outside Wolverhampton.

43 : The "new" double track Kingswinford Branch came into use on 11th January 1925 and new halts were provided at Brockmoor, Bromley, Pensnett and Gornal in preparation for the passenger service that was going to commence five months later. GW 57xx class 0-6-0PT, 9719, is seen here gliding past the remains of Brockmoor Halt on 3rd May 1956. The milepost on the up platform claims to be 144 mls. from London, but the halt was a mere 28 chains from Kingswinford Junction. (In 1984 the milepost was still in place, buried in dense undergrowth!) *(John Dew)*

44 : GW "Hall" class 4-6-0, 6931, *"Aldborough Hall"* approaches Pensnett Halt on 17th November 1962. Messrs. Gibbons, had their own siding on the down side (on the right). The up line is on the left, although at one time the two main running lines were those on the right of the picture! Close inspection of the grass on the left will reveal that the Corbyn's Hall Works of Messrs. Gibbons were also once served by rail. The whole scene changed once again in 1967 when the line was singled. *(John Dew)*

45 : Pensnett Halt seen through the arch of the bridge carrying the main Dudley-Kingswinford road in 1927. The line passing to the left of the halt was an up goods loop. The halt was only open for passenger traffic from 1925 to 1932 and was usually served by a GWR steam railcar. Trains often parted on the dip in the track at this point. *(H.J. Parker)*

46 : Pensnett Signal box, just at the southern end of the down platform of the halt. The box came into use on 1st January 1925 and was then called Pensnett South S.B. While the line was being rebuilt and extended trains had entered a section between Bromley Basin and Himley on possession of a wooden train staff. The box closed 17th December 1967, shortly after this photograph was taken. The top half of the box was moved to Bridgnorth station on the Severn Valley Railway. *(Paul Dorney)*

47 : North of the Dudley-Kingswinford Road the Kingswinford Branch entered an area that possesses a bewildering industrial history. The Stourbridge Extension Canal had made its way up to Shut End by 1840 to try and capture the traffic that was leaving this area via the Shut End Railway to Ashwood Basin on the Staffs & Worcs. Canal. Coal, ironstone and fireclay were all being worked in the area. The land seen on the left of this picture was occupied by Bradley's Shut End Ironworks, and later the Shut End Colliery Co. When the canal closed in 1938 the latter retained the right to transport between Shut End and Standhills Colliery by being allowed to run their engine over GWR metals!

By the early sixties the area was being developed as an industrial estate by Lunt, Comley & Pitt and the last two engines of the Shut End Colliery Co./Guy Pitt & Co. survived to work the lines into the estate (see opposite page). In this picture, taken late 1963, the Kingswinford Branch, and the line to Wombourn, are still in business and an engine is seen shunting the up sidings. On the left vans occupy the lines into the new trading estate. *(Viv Morgan)*

48 : The same view photographed on 15th June 1964. New sidings have been laid on the left of the picture to serve a new coal-concentration depot built by Lunt, Comley & Pitt, and opened on 1st May 1964. A small Ruston Hornsby four-wheel diesel loco is shunting their supplies of coal and the site is still being cleared. *(Viv Morgan)*

49 : This tele-photo view of the same location in 1983 reveals that the restless transformation of this landscape has never ceased. The line north of this point closed altogether on 1st April 1968, after the closure of Baggeridge Colliery and the coal concentration depot has become the sole reason for the branch's survival. A BR class 45 1-Co-Co-1 diesel locomotive is seen on the right, usually working the branch while on the "tripping" turn between Bescot and Stourbridge Junction, most of which is spent shunting Moor Lane Steel Terminal. The coal concentration depot has expanded and shunting is being performed by LCP's ex BR shunter (BR number 02003/D2868). *(Brian Robbins)*

50 : As stated on the opposite page, Guy Pitt & Co. took over the mining interests of John Bradley & Co. in the Shut End area in 1913. In May 1946 they acquired a Manning Wardle 0-6-0ST (Works number: 2025 of 1923). She had previously worked at Cadbury's works near Worcester, bearing the number "7". At Pensnett the loco became *"Winston Churchill"*. The loco survived long enough to be seen here working a train of container wagons on the short-lived railway system of the Pensnett Trading Estate, in 1961. In 1970 the loco was donated to the Black Country Museum and stood on the corner of the Museum's site for a few years until returning to the Pensnett Trading Estate where it has been externally restored and put on show. *(Viv Morgan)*

51 : Guy Pitt & Co.'s other long-surviving locomotive was a Barclay 0-6-0ST (Works number: 782 of 1896) named *"Peter"*, photographed in November 1963. This engine survives at the Ironbridge Gorge Museum, after standing out of use at Pensnett for a very long period. The name *"Peter"* was handed down to one of the "new" diesels. *(Viv Morgan)*

52 : Baggeridge Junction Signal Box marked the northern end of the double-tracked "Kingswinford Branch" and the beginning of the single-tracked "Wombourn Branch". It opened on 1st January 1925 when goods trains started using the new double line from there to Kingswinford Junction. When the Wombourn line closed, on 1st March 1965, the box remained open as the northern terminus of the branch and to command the surviving connection with the railway to Baggeridge Colliery. The box was destroyed by fire on 4th June 1967 and "officially closed" on 16th July 1967 when a new ground frame came into use at the junction. *(Edgar Rumble)*

53 : GW class 57xx 0-6-0PT, 8718, the last "square-cabbed" member of the class, waits to leave Baggeridge Junction for Stourbridge in June 1966, having just collected the wagons from the colliery engine. (See picture 176). *(Paul Dorney)*

The Wombourn branch was very late in arriving on the scene. As mentioned on page 17, it was built as the result of the GWR's original intention of linking Wolverhampton with Bridgnorth. By an Act of 11th July 1905 the GWR was given powers for such a line plus a branch from it, near Trysull, to the Kingswinford Branch. Three years later the scheme was revised and Wombourn itself was proposed as the junction, and in 1910 plans were made for the doubling of the Kingswinford Branch. In 1913 the attempt to reach Bridgnorth was postponed and construction began on the line as described here. The Kingswinford Branch was transformed and provided with four halts, the extension headed for Wombourn, via Himley, and thence to Wolverhampton via Tettenhall and halts at Penn and Compton. Perry & Co., of Bromley, acquired the contract for building the line and made good progress on the work until halted by the First World War. It was completed after the War by the GWR itself and opened on 11th May 1925. The passenger service lasted a mere seven years, ceasing on 31st October 1932, but goods traffic continued until 1st March 1965.

54 :Himley station under construction in 1914, looking towards Baggeridge Junction. The platform on the left was never used and when the permanent track was laid no loop was provided at this point. *(Ernest Milner, from the Collection of Bert Pritchard)*

55 : To build the Wombourn line Perry & Co. established their yard at Planks Lane, south of Wombourn. Their light railway ran almost the entire length of the proposed line and used nine locomotives, four of which are in this picture! In the foreground is *"David"*, a Manning Wardle 0-6-0ST (Works number: 774 of 1881). When Perry's work on the line ceased during the First World War *"David"* went to Guy Pitt & Co.'s Shut End Colliery railway and, apparently, was not scrapped until 1954.
(Ernest Milner, from the Collection of Bert Pritchard)

56 : Wombourn station, looking north, as it looked during its long sojourn as a passing place on a goods-only line. After the passenger service ceased in 1932 various enconomies were made in running the line. Wombourn signal box closed in 1935 but reopened again during the Second World War. The War saw the removal of the stations' nameboards although the posts survived, as in this picture. (The GWR spelt Wombourn without an "e"). After closure in 1965 the track was lifted and the buildings were left to decay. However, the building on the up platform, on the right, has been beautifully restored by South Staffordshire District Council and "reopened" on 2nd May 1981 as HQ of the footpath that uses the railway's trackbed. *(W.A. Camwell)*

57 : GW "Hall" class 4-6-0, 6944, *"Fledborough Hall"*, steams through Tettenhall on 29th April 1957 with a Crewe-Worcester freight. As at Himley, the up platform was never used and track never laid by it. The sleepers that appear alongside the up platform in this picture are there as a result of track renewal on the running line. Like Wombourn and Himley, Tettenhall had its own small goods yard, and an impressive red brick goods shed, but the line remained open for goods traffic mainly to provide a route for these "through-services" avoiding congestion at Wolverhampton and Dudley. In 1984 the building on the left is undergoing restoration but the footpath occupying the trackbed has become very overgrown. *(G.F. Bannister)*

58 : GW class 64xx 0-6-0PT, 6422, takes the double track that curves towards Oxley Middle Junction (and thence to Wolverhampton) on 26th April 1957 with a Saturdays Only working returning from Courtaulds' Siding. It has just passed Oxley Branch Junction where the single line from Tettenhall becomes two sets of double track forming a triangle with the main line from Wolverhampton to Shrewsbury. The double tracks on the right curve round to Oxley North Junction, facing Shrewsbury. Courtaulds' Siding (between Oxley Branch Junction and Tettenhall) was opened in August 1927 and the company had their own small internal system and locomotives (see picture 199). *(G.F. Bannister)*

59 : Aldersley viaduct under construction in 1914. The three-arch viaduct carried the double track curve from Oxley Branch Junction to Oxley Middle Junction over the Staffs & Worcs. Canal. Alongside, on the extreme left of the picture, is the viaduct carrying the main line to Shrewsbury. On the skyline, in the middle of the picture, is the outline of Oxley Engine Shed, opened in 1907.
(Ernest Milner, from the Collection of Bert Pritchard)

The Bumble Hole Line

The line from Blowers Green Junction to Old Hill was part of a scheme to link Dudley with Halesowen authorised by a West Midland Railway Act of 17th July 1862. The GWR inherited the scheme when it absorbed the West Midland but did not leap into action to build the line. When they did build it they arranged the junctions at Old Hill to the advantage of through-running to Snow Hill. The Dudley-Old Hill (and Old Hill-Halesowen) services commenced on 1st March 1878. The passenger service outlived the service on the West Midland line and the last train between Dudley and Old Hill ran on 13th June 1964. Goods trains ceased in 1968. In operating instructions the line was usually called the "Windmill End Branch" but most people knew it as the "Bumble Hole Line".

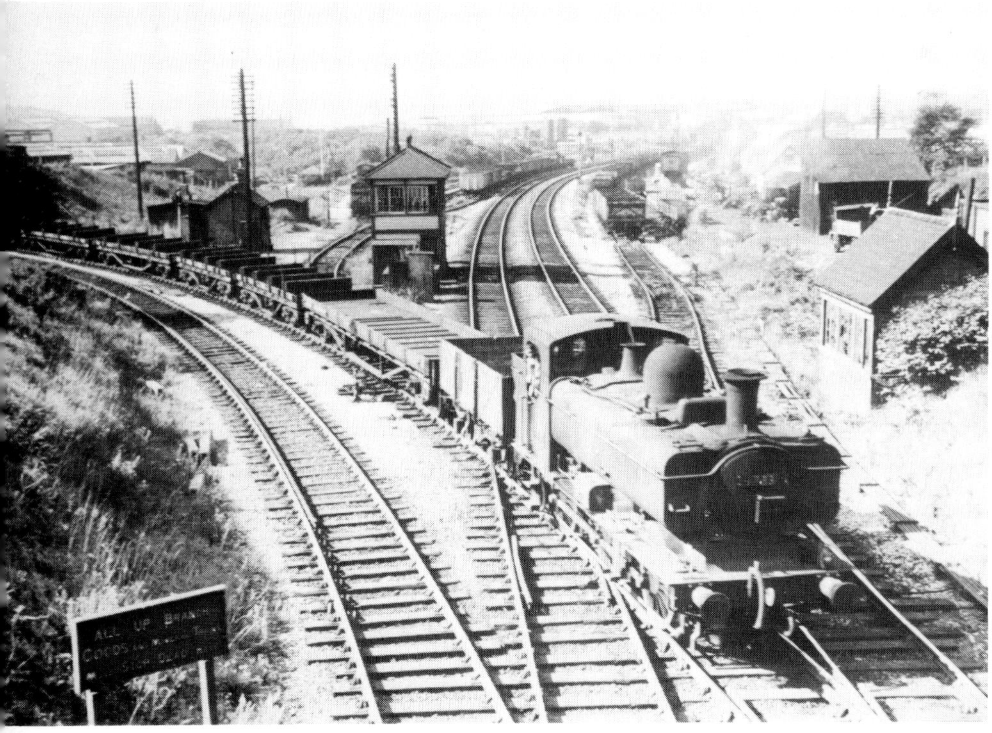

60 : A GW 57xx class 0-6-0PT, 9733, coming off the Bumble Hole line at Blowers Green Junction on 26th August 1964. 9733 was on yard duty and was just returning from Netherton Goods. Any engine consigned to this duty was called *"The Jacko"*. Note the warning to drivers about to join the line: "All up branch goods and mineral trains must stop dead here". *(Richard Taylor)*

61 : GW class 64xx, 0-6-0PT, 6424, leaving Baptist End Halt in wintry surroundings on 9th February 1963. The Bumble Hole line was latterly served only by trains in the morning and evening rush to and from work. Photographers hoping to catch the mid-day working on Saturdays were often jinxed by snow, rain and mist! Baptist End Halt was never staffed and such matters as attending to the oil in the signal lamps was the responsibility of the signalman at Windmill End Junction. *(John Dew)*

62 : GW streamlined diesel railcar, W14, entering Baptist End Halt in May 1956. This picture shows the original timber construction of the halts on this line. They were opened in March 1905 to coincide with the introduction of steam railcars on this service. It appears that they originally lacked shelter for intending passengers and the corrugated iron huts were erected after local protests. As on the Kingswinford Branch, these huts appear in photographs with a variety of roofs – pagoda-shaped, elliptical and, in this case, pitched! In 1957 the Bumble Hole Halts were replaced with new structures as seen in picture 61. *(Real Photographs)*

63 : A BR single-unit diesel railcar in the attractive green livery with "whiskers" approaches Baptist End Halt on a train from Old Hill on 31st August 1962, five years after the halt had been rebuilt. New "totem" nameboards, enamelled in W.R. colours, and cast concrete lamp posts completed the scene. In the background Windmill End Junction can be seen very clearly and the line diverging to the right was the Netherton Goods Branch (see page 25).
(P.J. Shoesmith)

64 : A BR single-unit diesel railcar, still in a green livery but no longer sporting "whiskers" runs through Windmill End Halt on its way to Old Hill early one evening in June 1964, shortly before the service ceased. Windmill End was reduced to the status of a halt in 1952 but during the 1957 rebuilding programme its former status and seniority (it was the only intermediate station on the line originally) were recognised with the erection of a more elaborate corrugated iron structure on the down platform! Prior to 1957 the wooden buildings had been quite ornate and impressive and the station possessed a footbridge. Close to the station was a canal crossroads, the entrance to Netherton canal tunnel, and Cobb's Engine House – used by the South Staffordshire Mines Drainage Co. to drain the local pits. Beyond the train in this picture the chimneys of Doultons pipe works can be seen.
(Ned Williams)

65 : A GW 64xx 0-6-0PT stands with an ex LMS push-pull unit at Darby End Halt with a train from Old Hill on 29th May 1964. Darby End Halt, perched on its embankment could be seen from Windmill End and it was an impressive sight to watch the little steam train wind its way up the valley in the shadow of the Rowley Hills between these lonely halts. *(P.J. Shoesmith)*

66 : Between Darby End and Old Hill High Street, the Bumble Hole line encountered Cox's Lane Crossing, sometimes spelt "Coxes Lane". At one time local people had expressed the wish for a halt to be built at this point, but one never materialised. Instead various goods sidings came and went, and on some occasions a banking engine rested here. The sidings on the up side of the line included one that served Messrs. Prestwick. On their weighbridge they had a large notice stating: "Engines, box vans, and brake-vans must not pass this board". This picture was taken in 1968 just after the line had closed. *(Paul Dorney)*

67 : An 0-6-0PT sets off from Old Hill High Street Halt for Dudley on 15th December 1962. The prevailing gradients of the Bumble Hole line were such that Cox's Lane was the lowest part of the line, and by the time the line reached Old Hill High Street Halt it was climbing towards its southern junction. High Street was not the principal street in Old Hill and, in fact, was quite a suitable backwater in which to find a GWR halt! *(John Dew)*

68 : GW class 64xx 0-6-0PT, 6403, has just arrived in Old Hill, having propelled its push-pull train from Dudley. After the departure of the train from Birmingham the Bumble Hole train would come back into the opposite platform and whisk one or two travellers away to those windswept halts. (There was no separate bay platform other than for Halesowen trains). Attractions at Old Hill included the nameboard and a delightfully decrepid wooden station building. *(John Dew)*

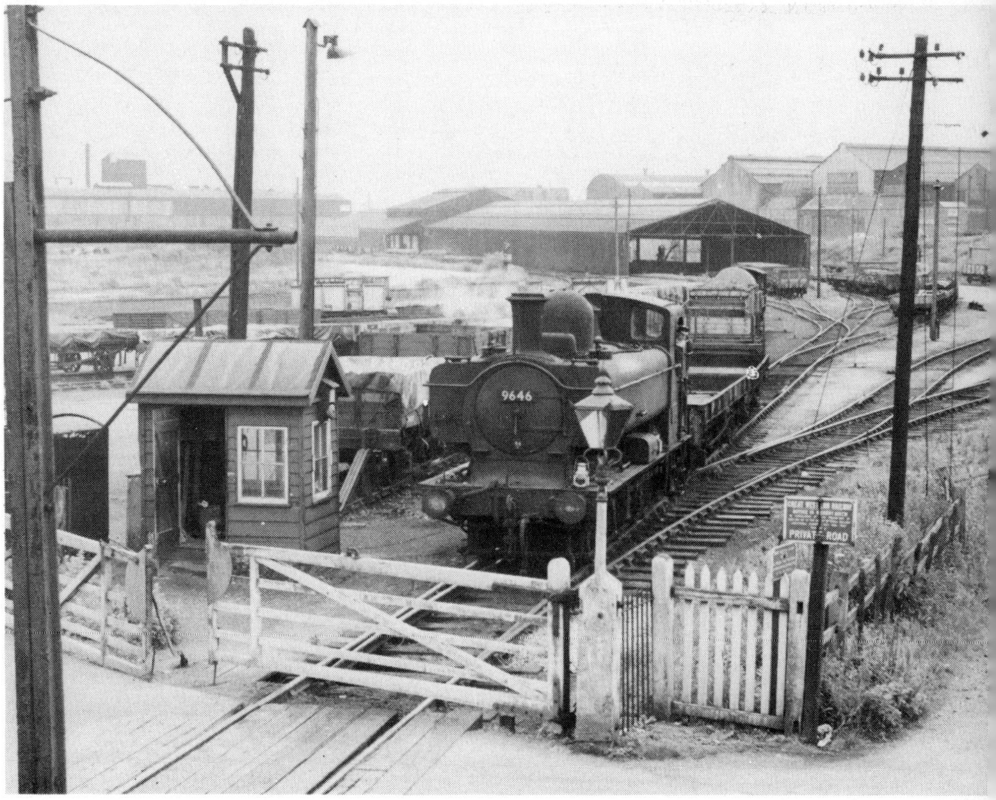

69 : The Netherton Goods Branch left the Bumble Hole line at Windmill End Junction, just south of Baptist End Halt (see picture 63) and quickly became a single line on a ruling grade of 1 in 51 for less than a mile to its terminus at Withymoor Basin. There were numerous sidings off the branch as it passed through an area with a very complex industrial history. It was a busy stretch of line and was by no means solely concerned with traffic that had to be transhipped to and from the canal. The large transhipment shed dominated the yard, as seen in this view from the footbridge in Northfield Road, but, as the importance of the basin declined, the yard became known simply as "Netherton Goods". The line opened on 10th March 1879 and closed on 5th July 1965. *(Ned Williams)*

70 : GW class 57xx 0-6-0PT, 9614, has just crossed Northfield Road Level Crossing on 10th June 1965, and drawn alongside the water tank. The water tank is now at Eardington on the Severn Valley Railway. *(Paul Dorney)*

71 : On the same occasion 0-6-0PT, 9614, is seen shunting in Netherton Goods Yard, coupled to the Blowers Green brakevan. The grass-covered tracks and the emptiness of the yard are signs that closure is imminent. The large shed in the background was demolished in 1967, but the arm of the canal was dredged about 1969 and has seen occasional use since then. *(Richard Taylor)*

72 : This view, from the main Dudley-Halesowen road, of the transhipment shed reveals the attractive wooden offices bearing the legend: "British Railways WR Netherton Goods". Note the lorry in its red and cream BR livery and the trailer awaiting its "mechanical horse".
(Bill Massey, Dudley Public Libraries)

73 : After shunting the yard 0-6-0PT, 9614, playing the role of *"The Jacko"*, returns to Blowers Green on 10th June 1965. Once the sidings were full and busy. Once the landscape was full of pits and furnaces, across the Bumble Hole to the Rowley Hills. *(Richard Taylor)*

74 : GW class 57xx 0-6-0PT, 3631, approaches Windmill End Junction on the Netherton Goods Branch with train no. *"T.31"* – a goods working from Netherton to Oxley Sidings, in April 1965. The distinctive GW brakevan, allocated to Blowers Green, seen in the other pictures is not on this train. Instead the guard is occupying an ex LMS van.
(Paul Dorney)

75 : Another similar "pannier", 3782, again on the T.31 trip, comes off the branch at Windmill End Junction, sometime during the branch's last few months of operation. *(Paul Dorney)*

76 : The GWR planned to make its way through the Black Country by backing, and later absorbing, the Birmingham, Wolverhampton and Dudley Railway. The BW & D opened on 14th November 1854 providing mixed-gauge tracks from Birmingham to Cannock Road, Wolverhampton. One of the stations opened on that date was Swan Village, but the BW & D certainly did not reach Dudley. The GWR finally reached Dudley from Birmingham by building a line from Swan Village to Horseley Fields Junction, on the South Staffordshire Line, over which it then had running powers to Dudley. This opened on 1st September 1866. Perhaps as a result of the awkward site of Dudley station, and perhaps as a result of Black Country folks' lack of interest in working in Birmingham this service never became intensively commuter-orientated, or perhaps it was a journey more sensibly accomplished by road. Often a railcar or push-pull train sufficed, and the service was withdrawn from 15th June 1964. This view of Dudley station shows the route that GWR trains had to take into an utterly LMS environment! The SSR tracks passed Dudley East Signal Box and went under Tipton Road. On the left of the box the LMS goods station can be seen. This later became a parcels depot for a time. LMS Ivatt 2-6-0, 46442 on a parcels train on 23rd July 1962. *(John Dew)*

77 : A 3-car Gloucester-built "Cross Country" DMU is seen approaching Dudley on 2nd May 1964 with the 5.40 p.m. ex Birmingham Snow Hill train. This view from the Tipton Road Bridge has altered considerably since then, although the SSR tracks are still in use. The long relief road has been lifted, the bridge that once carried a colliery tramroad has disappeared and a spectacular scrap yard occupies the LMS sidings site on the extreme left. *(Michael Mensing)*

78 : A GWR streamlined diesel railcar, W8, forms a Birmingham Snow Hill-Dudley train in the late 50s. It has just passed Dudley Port Low Level, without stopping. (It was not GWR policy to suggest to anyone that it might be possible to reach Birmingham via LMS services – despite the fact that passengers in the railcar had a clear view of the Stour Valley line crossing the back of this picture.) On the right is the siding used by the Palethorpes factory's traffic. *(Ted Higgs)*

79 : A BR (WR) Gloucester-built double-ended diesel railcar, 55006, pulling a driving trailer, passes through Dudley Port Low Level on the 6.00 p.m. ex Dudley train bound for Birmingham on 25th July 1959. The train will regain "proper" GWR tracks at Horseley Fields Junction and reach Swan Village via Great Bridge.
(Michael Mensing)

80 : The GWR climbed away from Horseley Fields Junction to reach Great Bridge South at a significantly higher altitude than the LMS station. The signal box, built in 1910, outlasted the withdrawal of the passenger trains in June 1964 as the line was retained for diversions, but finally closed on 10th August 1968. *(J.L. Smith)*

81 : GW class 56xx, 0-6-2T, 5658, brings a train from Birmingham across the bridge over New Road and into the remarkable station at Great Bridge South on 17th June 1963. *(P.J. Shoesmith)*

82 : Until recent times Swan Village had a station worthy of its rural-sounding name. In June 1957 GW railcar no. W8 arrives from Dudley on its way to Birmingham Snow Hill. On the right is the GWR main line stretching away to Hill Top Tunnel, just below the skyline. The rather new-looking footbridge linking the branch platforms was perhaps a sign the station was about to be modernised.
(Real Photographs)

83 : Swan Village was dominated by the Gas Works, with three distinctive gas holders, each of a different design. Today this gas holder, and the West Signal Box have gone. Railway tracks have vanished and part of the main line's formation has become a footpath. The "modern" West Box was built in 1952 and was only used for sixteen years. The enamel sign, still in place when photographed in 1970, directed passengers to a new main station building just barely visible on the extreme right of picture 84.
(Roger Crombleholme)

84 : GW class 51xx 2-6-2T, 4158, halts at the branch platform at Swan Village and waits to depart for Dudley in 1963, a year before the service was withdrawn. The main line platforms at Swan Village saw the passing of fewer and fewer trains until the local passenger service between Snow Hill and Wolverhampton was withdrawn in 1972.
(P.J. Shoesmith)

G. W. R.

Swan Village

Dudley Port Low Level (SSR) opened on 1st May 1850. The High Level Station (LNWR) opened on 1st July 1852. Meanwhile the SSR had obtained powers to build a connection between the two levels. On 2nd January 1854 a short line from the SSR at Sedgeley Junction up to the High Level was brought into use. At one time trains ran from Birmingham to Kidderminster via Dudley using this spur but eventually its passenger services were reduced to the *"Dasher"* – a frequent push-pull train operating between Dudley and the bay platform at Dudley Port. Ancient LNWR Webb 2-4-2T locomotives usually worked the *"Dasher"* although modern Ivatt 2-6-2T's were also seen. After 1958 the *"Dasher"* was a DMU doing the one remaining timetabled trip between other duties. It ran for the last time on 13th June 1964, and the connection was severed a month later.

WANTED

Good photos of the *"Dasher"* for Vol. II.

85 : The water tower at Dudley Port is clearly visible in picture 79, and in this picture forms the background to the signal at the end of the down platform. The main signal guarded the Dudley line while the one on the left guarded a carriage siding, the one on the right a goods loop between here and Watery Lane. Beyond the canal can be seen the embankment taking the line down to Sedgeley Junction (LNWR spelling). *(Ted Higgs)*

86 : The board above the seat on the bay platform made it quite clear that LNWR/LMS passengers could use the *"Dasher"* to reach the GWR services from Dudley as well as the South Staffs Line from Low Level. *(Ted Higgs)*

87 & 88 : The Palethorpes siding at Sedgeley Junction provided traffic in the company's own distinctive vans, often seen at Dudley and at Dudley Port. M38876M is a bogie example, M38735M, a six-wheeler. *(Ted Higgs)*

The South Staffordshire Railways was incorporated in 1846 and set out to build a line from Wichnor Junction on the Midland Railway, near Burton, to the OWWR at Dudley, via Walsall. The first section of the SSR to be completed was from Bescot to Walsall, in 1847. Walsall to Wichnor opened 9th April 1849. The line from Walsall (Pleck Junction) to Dudley opened for goods traffic on 1st March 1850, and for passengers on 1st May, despite the fact that passenger facilities at Dudley were not completed. (Dudley did not acquire an adequate "joint" station for some time).

The SSR was leased to the LNWR in 1861 and absorbed in 1867, bringing the LNWR and the GWR alongside one another in Dudley.

Although passenger services between Dudley and Walsall ceased on 6th July 1964, the line has survived, and seen a number of changes in the last two decades.

89 : A two car DMU stands at the LMS platform at Dudley station awaiting departure for Walsall at 4.18 p.m. on 26th April 1962. *(John Dew)*

90 : A two car Park Royal DMU forms the 4.18 p.m. Dudley to Walsall train approaching Dudley Port on 25th July 1959. This interesting view has changed considerably. On the right can be seen the broad sweep of the embankment climbing from Sedgeley Junction to Dudley Port High Level. Both the embankment and the allotments have now disappeared beneath a new housing estate. On the left is the Palethorpes Siding glimpsed in picture 78, and, in the distance, the goods transhipment shed used by Palethorpes. Castle Hill, Dudley, forms the skyline. *(Michael Mensing)*

91 : On 2nd August 1963 a 2 car DMU, in the later livery, enters the down platform at Dudley Port Low Level on its way to Walsall. This picture complements picture 79 in what it shows of the High Level and also shows the station building (SSR?) on this platform. The abutments of the early tramroad bridge are also clearly visible. *(P.J. Shoesmith)*

92 : BR class 45 diesel 1-Co-Co-1, 45049, passes through the site of Dudley Port Low Level on 6th June 1980. All trace of buildings and platforms have gone in this view facing the opposite direction to the previous picture. One local landmark that was familiar to many travellers was the legend on the far embankment: "Next stop – Dudley Zoo".
(Robert Selvey)

93 : Great Bridge North was a fairly modest station, only a hundred yards from its GWR counterpart. Most photographers stood on the footbridge (see below) but this picture was taken from the point where the footpath down to the station reached New Road, thus placing the station in its setting. (The remains of the path are still visible but the station has disappeared. The goods yard on the right has recently returned to life for a short time.) The 2 car DMU is seen leaving for Dudley and is about to pass Great Bridge Signal Box, on 17th May 1963.
(P.J. Shoesmith)

94 : LMS 2-4-2T, 46712, calls at Great Bridge North on 12th May 1950 with the push-pull train bound for Dudley. Note the boiler on the wagon on the extreme right. The substantial goods shed has been demolished but the tanks (Ratcliffe's) in the left background still form a distinctive part of the local landscape. *(Real Photographs)*

95 : BR class 20 Bo-Bo diesel, 20 084, driven by George Sparry, draws an engineers train across Eagle Crossing on 21st March 1984, watched by pilotman Johnny Butler. On the far side of the crossing the up line is being re-laid following the collapse of a culvert at this point in December 1963. Single line working is in force and the train has to be drawn clear of the line for a freight from Bescot to come past. The modern box at Eagle Crossing looks after a stretch of line once controlled by the boxes, here, at Horseley Fields, Great Bridge (Town Bridge) and Goldshill, and was opened about 1970. *(Ned Williams)*

96 : Goldshill Crossing, overlooked by the CEGB power station at Ocker Hill, was one of those places that was rarely photographed. Its primitive box had few modern comforts and was generally disliked by signalmen. Thankfully, for posterity, on one occasion the relief signalman photographed his new car by the crossing as the box and the traditional wooden gates have now gone. A pair of modern aluminium gates protect the crossing today – and may outlive the power station! *(Edgar Rumble)*

97 : BR class 37 diesel Co-Co, 37079, crosses the Tame Valley Canal by Goldshill Crossing on 2nd May 1984, and heads for Wednesbury. A few days later one of the chimneys on the power station began to shrink as demolition began. *(Ned Williams)*

98 : Ocker Hill Power Station again forms the backdrop as BR class 45 1-Co-Co-1 diesel, 45116, approaches Wednesbury on 14th May 1984. On the left, above the fourth and fifth wagons of the train can be seen the trackbed of the Princes End line and the surviving tracks of the short branch to the oil-fired standby power station at Ocker Hill. The larger coal-fired station, whose cooling towers can be seen for miles, has been closed for some time. On the right are the "Exchange Sidings" – for "exchange" between GWR and LMS systems, and presently providing access to Wednesbury Steel Terminal (see pictures 123 & 124). *(Ned Williams)*

99 : The same train, behind 45116, passes Wednesbury No. 1 signal box, crosses Potter Lane, and rushes through the remains of Wednesbury Town Station. How this view has changed is made clear by comparison with the next picture. The landmark that dominates this view of the station, the steeple of St. John's Church, is also likely to disappear shortly. This picture and the previous one were taken from the trackbed of the former GWR main line (see picture 122). *(Ned Williams)*

100 : LMS class G2A 0-8-0, 48930, at Wednesbury Town with an SLS special train on 2nd June 1962. The footbridge at the far end of the platform, and the one by the Potter Lane Crossing from which this picture was taken have since disappeared, along with the timber yard on the right, the island platform from which Princes End trains once left and the semaphore signals. *(John Dew)*

101 : While the SLS special paused at Wednesbury Town on 2nd June 1962 a Dudley-Walsall 2 car DMU passed through and is photographed here from the opposite end of the station, illustrating that the steps from the footbridge led to a building in the apex of the SS line platform and the Darlaston loop platform. *(P.J. Shoesmith)*

102 : Two 3 car B'ham RCW DMUs forming a Manchester-Birmingham train diverted via the SS line on Sunday 11th April 1965, because of electrification work at Wolverhampton. It is seen passing Mesty Croft just outside Wednesbury. *(Michael Mensing)*

103 : BR class 46 1-Co-Co-1 diesel 46016 crosses the low viaduct near Wood Green on 24th 1975 as it approaches Bescot. On the right, just above the viaduct, the parapet of the M6 motorway can be seen. A maze of railway lines, and motorway sliproads fill the Tame Valley at this point. *(Robert Selvey)*

104 : LMS class G2A 0-8-0, 48930, takes the SLS Special of 2nd June 1962 over the curve from Bescot to the South Staffordshire line, rarely used by passenger trains, and now much hidden beneath the arches of the M6 motorway. *(P.J. Shoesmith)*

105 : A BR 2 car DMU stands at Walsall station on Saturday, 4th July 1964, forming the last train on this service to Dudley. There was no Sunday service and the line was closed to passenger traffic as from 6th July. *(John Dew)*

106 : In June 1949, the Walsall-Dudley push pull train (the *"Dasher"* or the *"Dodger"*) was in the hands of LMS Webb 2-4-2T, 46757, at Walsall. *(Real Photographs)*

The LNWR's direct service between Wolverhampton and Walsall was able to commence on 1st March 1881 once the Pleck curve and the Wolverhampton-Portobello Junction lines had been built. Between these curves the service used the Grand Junction Railway's line opened as early as 4th July 1837.

107 : Although this passenger service survived until 18th January 1965 few photographers seemed interested in Darlaston or Willenhall. This picture of a 2 car DMU entering Darlaston, on 2nd August 1963, shows that the station and box (just visible behind the train!) were definitely worth photographing and were good examples of the LNWR's timber-built buildings. When the GJR's station on this site opened it was known as both James Bridge and Darlaston. In 1863 it was renamed simply "James Bridge" to distinguish it from the new "Darlaston" on the loop from Wednesbury. After a couple of modifications, after the loop lost its passenger service, this station simply became "Darlaston" once more. *(P.J. Shoesmith)*

108 : On the same day a similar BR 2 car DMU is seen leaving Willenhall with a through train from Wolverhampton to Burton. Between 1837 and 1965 this station had also seen one or two changes made to its name, and for a while it was known as Willenhall (Bilston Street) to distinguish it from the station on Midland line. *(P.J. Shoesmith)*

109 : As can be seen in the above picture, Willenhall used two of the attractive LNWR timber buildings at platform level but behind the down platform an original GJR building stood until the station's closure and demolition. In this picture of that building its similarity with the GJR building at Wednesfield Heath is apparent. (The distinctive lintels must have been a GJR "trademark".) It presumably dates from 1837 and contrasts with the timber building probably dating from 1881 and the enamelled station nameboard in glowing BR Midland Region maroon. *(Ted Higgs)*

110 : The 5.52 p.m. Wolverhampton-Walsall push pull train in the days of steam. LMS 6704 is seen propelling a two coach push pull train of LNWR vintage, and hauling a horse box, approaching Portobello Junction on 30th July 1947. The "new" curve from Wolverhampton High Level descends quite dramatically at this point to join the former GJR main line. Some indication of the level of the latter can be grasped when it is realised that the parapet of a bridge *over* the GJR line can be seen on the extreme right. *(Tim Shuttleworth)*

111 : A BR 2 car Metro-Cammell DMU approaches Wolverhampton High Level from Walsall on 10th April 1964. It will join the Stour Valley main line at Crane Street Junction, at the top right hand corner of the picture, after passing over the bridge above the tunnels immediately south of Low Level station. The GWR tracks, as seen through a telefoto lens from the Low Level station, are no more but the LNWR's line to Portobello is electrified and carries freight and diverted passenger services. *(P.J. Shoesmith)*

Wolverhampton Byways

At Wolverhampton the railway systems of the Black Country first converge and then diverge as they head to the north and west. As the GWR lines have declined and disappeared in a rationalisation that has favoured the LMS lines many interesting byways have come and gone. From 1972 onwards even the Low Level station itself became a byway!

After 4th March 1968 the lines from Stafford Road Junction and Bushbury junction to the Low Level were officially closed. On 6th October 1969 they were both reopened to the point where they both met, at Cannock Road Junction, to provide a route of Merry-Go-Round coal trains to reach Ironbridge Power Station. The former main line and the "connecting line" therefore became a new byway, particularly after the line south of Cannock Road was severed in January 1970 and the junction (where MGR trains had to reverse) was remodelled. In August 1983 this was replaced by the opening of a "brand new byway", the Oxley Chord, cutting out the need for a reversal at Cannock Road!

112 : A class 47 diesel loco brings an empty MGR train under the Stour Valley line viaduct and onto the new Oxley Chord line as an Inter-city train passes overhead. On the left is the trackbed of the line into Stafford Road Shed, on the right: the track of the line to Cannock Road Junction. *(Ned Williams)*

113 : Another byway was the line to Victoria Basin, once the Shrewsbury and Birmingham's approach to Wolverhampton, opened in 1849. Once the S & BR's connection with the LNWR was severed, in 1859, the line became a goods only branch from Stafford Road Junction to the canal basin and Herbert Street Goods Depot. (S & BR passenger trains had been diverted to Low Level since 1854). Ironically, in 1966, the junction was reinstated and part of this byway became a main line again, but on 13th November 1954, when this photograph was taken the passage of this SLS "special" to Victoria Basin was something very unusual. GWR 0-4-2T, 1438 and trailers 45 and 61 were charted by the SLS to celebrate the centenary of the opening of the GWR line from Snow Hill to Wolverhampton. The Mayor of Wolverhampton poses on the footplate of 1438 at Victoria Basin. *(Phil Lycett)*

114 : The canal basin at Monmore Green was originally the terminus of a tramroad from the Chillington Ironworks. When the OWWR opened its goods station at Walsall Street its tracks reached the canal at the adjoining Shrubbery Basin. In 1902 the LNWR began using the Monmore Green basin, having built a loop from the Stour Valley line to reach it. The OWWR goods yard was remodelled in 1966 to become a steel terminal and in recent times this has been reached from the former LNWR's Monmore Green Branch. On 6th June 1984, 08 466 stands in the yard outside the old Monmore Green canal transhipment shed, now used as overflow yard for the steel terminal. In the foreground is a new branch to the British Oxygen Company's depot, opened 24th September 1971. *(Ned Williams)*

115 : BR class 40, 40174, clears the bridge over the Wolverhampton-Bilston Road to Monmore Green Junction in October 1982 while coming to collect a train of BOC wagons, collected from the BOC depot by an 08 shunter. *(Ned Williams)*

The Wolverhampton & Walsall Railway was a local company, incorporated on 29th June 1865. Four further Acts of Parliament, and seven and a half years later it opened on 1st November 1872. Both the LNWR and the Midland were going to work trains over it, and in 1875 it was bought by the LNWR and then sold, a year later to the Midland, although trains continued to use the LNWR station at Wolverhampton. Passenger services ceased on the line on 5th January 1931 and when the line was "broken" by the building of the M6, in 1964, it became two goods-only byways: Wolverhampton to Wednesfield and Walsall to Birchills Power Station. Now those two lines have closed.

116 : Two LNWR class G2a 0-8-0s at Heath Town Junction. (The signal box, of typical Midland design, can just be seen on the left). At this point the LNWR's 1881 curve to Portobello Junction curved away just before the W & WR's line is met by a connecting spur, seen in the foreground, that leads to the Midland's Wednesfield Road Goods Depot and the GWR's Low Level Station. *(Phil Lycett)*

117 : An 08 0-6-0 diesel shunter returns from Wednesfield on 17th March 1981, after shunting what was probably the last train to use the branch. On the right, almost beneath the loco, is the retaining wall above the GJR's tunnel at Wednesfield Heath and the loco is about to cross the Wyrley & Essington Canal on a bridge that is a monument to the art of bricklaying "on the skew". *(Ned Williams)*

118 : Wednesfield Station in February 1950. The station buildings on this line were all of this pattern, but as its passenger service was withdrawn so early, the stations were seldom photographed.
(Real Photographs)

119 : Once the M6 had bisected the W & WR's line the western half saw little further use and was closed on 4th October 1965. It was reopened in 1970 to serve the Weldless Steel Tube Co.'s large works at Wednesfield and was used by block trains delivering steel from Round Oak Steel Works. Here, closer to the site of Wednesfield station, a siding descended the side of the embankment to serve the Ductile Steel Company, who kept their engine in the shed on the extreme left of the picture. (Photo taken 4th July 1976). *(Robert Selvey)*

120 : Ductile Steel Co.'s 0-4-0 Ruston Hornsby diesel is about to shunt six bogie bolster wagons of steel bars to the company's overhead crane for unloading on 10th March 1981. The running lines, significantly higher than the sidings quickly singled and meandered back across Wednesfield Heath to Heath Town Junction. *(Philip Barnard)*

121 : BR class 08 0-6-0 diesel, 08765 returns to Wolverhampton after delivering steel bars to Ductile Steel Co., Wednesfield. Beyond the Neachells Lane bridge the line still stretches to the Weldless Steel Tube Co., but is unused. This picture was taken 10th March 1981, a week later the line appeared to be used for the last time, but at the time of writing the track is still in situ. *(Philip Barnard)*

NB. The other end of the W & WR is mentioned in the section devoted to Birchills Power Station on page 65 (pictures 193 & 194).

122 : Immediately south of Wednesbury Town the "Exchange Sidings" curve away on the down side. BR class 25/3 Bo-Bo diesel, 25273 backs into the sidings with a down freight in order to collect more wagons before continuing to Bescot on 27th June 1977. In the background the ex GWR main line is seen crossing the SS line and appears to be used for storing wagons, although still open, at that time, to Black Lake. (See picture 127). The bridge has now been removed.
(Michael Mensing)

123 : The Exchange Sidings now form an approach to Wednesbury Steel Terminal, the overhead crane of which is seen in the background of this picture. BR class 47, Co-Co diesel, 47224 brings two Rail Freight vans down from the Steel Terminal on 8th June 1984. In the centre background the last surviving buildings of the Patent Shaft complex can be seen, now Wiggins Alloys, and the open mineral wagons on the extreme right background are occupying sidings on the site of Wednesbury Central (GWR) station.
(Ned Williams)

124 : BR class 45 1-Co-Co-1 diesel, 45012 stands at Wednesbury Steel Terminal on 14th May 1984 while, a mile or two away, the Chairman of BRB, Bob Reid, opens Sandwell & Dudley station! On the right the line continues to Moxley. *(Ned Williams)*

125 : BR class 47, Co-Co diesel, 47195, approaches Wednesbury Steel Terminal, seen in the distance on the right. It is returning "light engine" from Wolverhampton Steel Terminal, to which it has delivered a train, on 29th September 1980. Perhaps it is surprising to think steel still reached the Terminal via the old GWR main line even into the eighties! The overgrown track in the foreground was once a siding serving the Willingsworth Iron Works. *(Robert Selvey)*

126 : BR class 08 0-6-0 diesel shunter, 08 603, halts at the present terminus of the line from Wednesbury : the scrapyard of Messrs. Norton Barrow (Metals) Ltd., seen from Loxdale Road, Moxley on 7th June 1984. Behind the shunter, and its train of one mineral wagon, is the now empty trackbed of the former GWR main line. The track occupied by the train was formerly a down relief goods loop, brought into use in 1917, which extended all the way from Wednesbury to Bilston. (It is visible in the picture above). *(Ned Williams)*

127 : A BR class 25 Bo-Bo diesel pushes a p.w. train back to Wednesbury from Black Lake on 22nd October 1975, and is about to cross the river Tame. The LCP coal yard at Black Lake became the terminus of this byway (again once part of the GWR main line) once the line south of Swan Village crossing was taken out of use in 1972. Since then the coal yard has closed and the track has been lifted. *(Roger Monk)*

128 : Another byway from Wednesbury, that barely survives, is the line that ran alongside the Princes End line to some sidings at the oil-fired stand by power station at Ocker Hill. By the summer of 1983 the line was buried beneath deep vegetation but the track was cleared in the autumn and on 16th April 1984, BR class 47 Co-Co diesel 47 001 used the line to deliver oil during the early weeks of the Miners' Strike. *(Ned Williams)*

129 : The branch from Wednesbury Town to Darlaston was double track throughout and left from its own platforms at the Walsall end of Wednesbury Town Station. It was constructed by the LNWR while still leasing the SSR and opened on 14th September 1863. Defeated by the success of local tramways its passenger service was withdrawn on 1st November 1887, but the line itself lasted more than a century. As the line left Wednesbury it passed a yard in which Messrs. R.A. Giblin conducted a scrap metal business in and around the LNWR goods shed. In this picture, taken 7th December 1975, their Baguely shunting engine (works number: 2107 of 1937) can be seen plus the two small diesels that are still there today (summer 1984!). *(Robert Selvey)*

130 : The Darlaston-Wednesbury line was closed in stages. Darlaston-Fallings Heath closed in 1963, from there to Patent Shaft sidings closed on 1st January 1968 but from those sidings to Wednesbury was retained until the steel works closed in mid 1980. BR class 25, Bo-Bo diesel, then numbered D7629, later numbered 25279, approaches Patent Shaft Sidings, as seen from the Holyhead Road, about 1967 with a weed-killing train. *(Roger Crombleholme)*

131 : The other loop constructed by the LNWR while leasing the SSR was the Princes End line. The line left the SS line just south of Wednesbury and ran through Ocker Hill and Princes End to Bloomfield Junction, Tipton, on the Stour Valley main line and was opened on 14th September 1863. It closed to passengers on 1st November 1890 but a service was restored on 1st July 1895 only to be withdrawn again on 1st January 1916. It was a useful line for coping with diversions and BR class 40 1-Co-Co-1 diesel D225 (40 025) *"Lusitania"* is seen here on Sunday, 29th September 1963 having just left Bloomfield Junction with a Birmingham-Liverpool train. Electrification between Wolverhampton and Stafford had sent it onto the Princes End line and thence to Walsall and Rugeley. *(Michael Mensing)*

132 : Princes End (LNWR) was one of several stations serving the Tipton area, and one of two to include the place in its name. The neat LNWR signal box, seen in June 1976, controlled the level crossing, which by then had become lifting barriers, and controlled access to track from there to Wednesbury which had been singled. When the line finally closed, or faded away, in the early 1980s, the box was demolished. *(Keith Hodgkins)*

133 : BR class 25 Bo-Bo diesel, 25209, passes the site of Ocker Hill station on 30th October 1980 with a train of scrap metal that has had to crawl at less than 10 m.p.h. across the unstable embankment between there and Princes End. Since the track has been lifted the embankment has been removed to try and quell its underground fires! *(Robert Selvey)*

134 : BR class 25 Bo-Bo diesel, 25195, approaches Ocker Hill Power Station on 26th September 1980 with only a brake van for company. Perhaps the guard is contemplating what a loss to the landscape we will suffer when the cooling towers are demolished. *(Robert Selvey)*

The Oldbury Branch was the result of plans to build the Dudley & Oldbury Railway, incorporated on 21st September 1873. In 1876 the GWR agreed to operate the line once it was built, and in 1881 it changed its name to the Oldbury Railway. It opened to goods on 7th November 1884 to a canal basin at Oldbury, and to passengers on 1st May 1885 when a new junction station was opened at Langley Green, east of the earlier station. It amalgamated with the GWR on 1st July 1894 and in 1905 was one of the several local branches to see the introduction of GWR steam railcars. Its passenger service could not compete with road transport, however, and it ceased on 3rd March 1915. The branch remained open to goods traffic until 7th September 1964. Since then a short section of the branch, singled since 1971 has continued to serve Albright and Wilson's chemical plant.

135 : An enthusiasts' special stands at the site of Oldbury station, a few hundred yards short of the canal basin and goods yard terminus of the line on 17th March 1962. The signal box, that once stood on the station's down platform remained open until 7th September 1964. *(John Dew)*

136 : Today the Oldbury branch still carries wagons to the sidings of Messrs. Albright and Wilson. BR class 31 AIA–AIA diesel, 31 198 leaves Langley Green on 11th June 1984 with a short train of green "Procor" tankers carrying Trichlorethylene. The single-line token is somewhere in mid-air between the signalman and driver as the train crawls past the disused passenger platforms. Note that the Stourbridge Junction line, in the background, still enjoys the sight of some lower-quadrant signals. *(Ned Williams)*

137 : BR class 25, Bo-Bo diesel, 25253, takes the green tankers down the Oldbury branch on 28th August 1981. It will have to reverse the train into Messrs. Albright and Wilson's chemical plant, which dominates the skyline. (There is also traffic in white chlorine tankers). *(Robert Selvey)*

Langley Green is the departure point for one other "byway" service as well as the Oldbury Branch. It also serves as a reversing point for cement-carrying trains bound for Handsworth. These trains arrive from Galton Junction and reverse at Langley Green into the Rood End Yard. The engine then runs round and takes the train back the way it has just come as far as Smethwick West where it takes the surviving single track to Handsworth Junction and thence to the Blue Circle Cement Depot.

138 : BR class 47, Co-Co diesel, 47 376, having reversed at Langley Green, brings its train of PCR cement-tankers, through the site of the Hawthorns Halt on its way to Handsworth on 19th May 1984. The Hawthorns Halt opened 25th December 1931 to serve the adjacent Albion football ground when required. The centre background was the site of Sandwell Colliery and the void on the right was once the GWR main line! Handsworth Junction Signal Box stood in the left foreground of this picture, closed in 1972. *(Ned Williams)*

139 : 47376 shunts at Handsworth Cement Sidings on 19th May 1984, as seen from the site of the former Queens Head Signal Box. *(Ned Williams)*

140 : 47376 returns to Smethwick West Junction from Handsworth on 19th May 1984. It is seen crossing the Birmingham Canal and the Stour Valley electrified main line, a hundred yards from the junction. In the background is Telford's magnificent Galton Bridge. Originally trains from the Stourbridge Extension line took the line to Handsworth Junction and thence to Snow Hill, but, since March 1967, these services have run to Birmingham New Street via a reopened Galton Junction. It is interesting to note that the cement train will have to work "wrong line" from Smethwick West to Langley Green before reversing yet again. *(Ned Williams)*

Halesowen Station was the meeting point of two separate railways: the GWR branch from Old Hill, and the Halesowen Railway (GW & Midland Joint) from Halesowen Junction on the Midland main line near Northfield. The GWR line was the result of an Act passed on 17th July 1862 for the West Midland Railway authorising the construction of line from Dudley to Halesowen via Old Hill (see page 22). The line opened on 1st March 1878.

The Halesowen Railway's earliest authorisation was on 5th July 1865, but it did not acquire that name until a third Act was passed in 1876. The Midland and the GWR had agreed to work the line but had no direct part in its slow and tedious construction. Several Acts and several years later the line opened on 10th September 1883.

Opposite page :

141 : Halesowen station, about 1910, showing trains of both companies. On the right a GWR steam railcar has arrived from Old Hill, while a Midland Railway train behind a Johnson 0-4-4T stands in the centre stabling line awaiting its turn to take the "Joint" line southwards to Northfield. Note the station garden in the foreground and the neat platform-level signal box on the right. *(Miss Payton)*

142 : This time a GWR 0-6-05T stands in the centre road at Halesowen while the station is decorated to celebrate a royal occasion (possibly the Coronation of King George V?). *(Miss Payton)*

This page :

143 : GWR steam railcar number 36 and railway staff posed at southern end of Halesowen station. Railcar services commenced in 1905. Public passenger services ceased on 5th December 1927. Behind the roof of the signal box can be seen the premises of Messrs. Rose Brothers. (General, Major, Captain and Baron Rose!). Later Walter Somers Ltd. dominated the station's backdrop. *(Miss Payton)*

144 : Mr. Payton, Halesowen's Edwardian station master, took great pride in the station's appearance, the cleanliness of the railcars and the brightness of the station garden, for which he regularly won prizes. He was a parish councillor and lived in a house overlooking the station. *(Miss Payton)*

145 : Signalman John James in Halesowen Signal Box on 2nd June 1962, on the arrival of a SLS DMU rail-tour. He had just finished painting the white edge to the station platform seen in picture 146, and his box was about to be invaded by enthusiasts! *(Collection of John James)*

G.W.R.

Halesowen

G.W.R.

Old Hill

146 : A BR 3 car DMU forms the SLS special train that called at Halesowen on 2nd March 1962, referred to in the caption to picture 145. Mr. Payton's station garden, on the extreme left, is now overgrown but the GWR wooden station name board is still propped by the platform fence. *(John Dew)*

147 : An LMS Ivatt class 2 2-6-0, 46522, resplendent in fully lined green livery, stands at the north end of Halesowen station with an SLS special on 2nd November 1963. The train was organised as a farewell to the Harborne and Halesowen branches, and was worked with an engine at each end (46421 was on the other end). Very few photographs taken at Halesowen show the goods shed, on the left, or the coal handling machinery on the right. *(John Dew)*

148 : Midland Railway class 2F 0-6-0, 58271, passes under the bridge near the foot of Mucklow Hill while leaving Halesowen on another SLS rail-tour which ran on 30th May 1959. Behind the engine's chimney it might just be possible to see the top of the GWR water tank. Track remained in situ so that engines could reach this tank until the end of steam. *(John Dew)*

149 : South of Halesowen the railway was originally operated jointly by the Midland Railway and the GWR, although the stations had a distinctly Midland look about them. An ex Midland Railway 2F 0-6-0, 58168, is seen here at Hunnington Station on 2nd June 1956. The small corrugated iron goods shed in the yard was erected to deal with traffic from the famous Bluebird Toffee factory. *(John Dew)*

150 : The most famous feature of the Halesowen Railway was the trestle viaduct at Dowery Dell, between Hunnington and Rubery. Regular passenger trains ceased to traverse it in 1919, but two years earlier special workmen's trains had started to run to the Austin Motor Co. at Longbridge and these trains continued to cross the viaduct until 1st September 1958. The viaduct was demolished in 1965. On 10th May 1957 0-6-0PT, 7448, crosses the viaduct with the 5. 9. p.m. ex Longbridge. *(John Dew)*

151 : Ex Midland Railway class 2F 0-6-0, 58138, passes Rubery station on 3rd September 1955. Note the driver is about to pass the token to the signalman and the MR signal standing on the opposite platform. *(John Dew)*

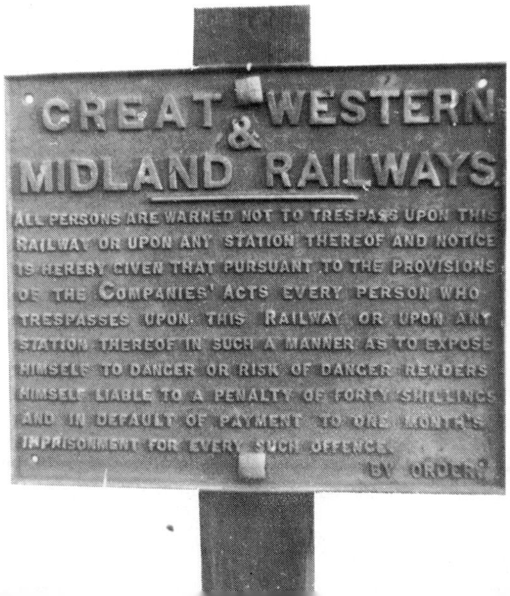

152 : A "Joint" cast iron trespass warning. *(John Dew)*

153 : To avoid congestion at Longbridge it was necessary to pass workmen's trains at Rubery. On the right GWR 0-6-0PT 1835 enters Rubery with a full train bound for Old Hill, while, on the left, 0-6-0PT 1745, with open cab, waits to take its empty train down to Longbridge. The date is 11th September 1947 but the open cabbed pannier and the celestory coach have a nineteenth century appearance!
(P.J. Garland, from the Collection of R.S. Carpenter)

154 : Just south of Rubery was Frogmill Crossing, and, at one time a line had run from there to Hollymoor Hospital. In later years this small lever frame operated the signals guarding the crossing. *(John Dew)*

155 : Longbridge Station in 1921, looking towards Halesowen and surrounded by the Austin Motor Co. works. Later, extensive shelters were built on these platforms and although the northbound workmen's trains ceased in 1958, the southbound trains to New Street continued until January 1960. Although not remotely part of the Black Country this station is part of Black Country history as so many Blackcountrymen used the workmen's service to work at Longbridge.
(Collection of R.S. Carpenter)

156 : Ex MR class 2F 0-6-0, 58271, reaches the southern extremity of the Halesowen Railway at Halesowen Junction, with the SLS special of 30th May 1959. The new Longbridge station is just to the north of this junction.
(Real Photographs)

157 : The branch from Halesowen to Halesowen Basin was authorised by the GWR (General Powers) Act of 2nd August 1898 and was opened on 2nd April 1902. From Canal Basin Junction (controlled by a ground frame) it climbed on a sharp curve round the works of Walter Somers Ltd. and reversed into sidings and transhipment shed at the basin. At one time sidings also served Coombs Wood Colliery, and the line served Walter Somers Ltd. The steam workings on the branch survived almost to the end of the steam era and the line closed on 1st October 1969. GWR 57xx 0-6-0PT, 4698, in grimy condition, and without number plates, approaches the basin in 1968. *(John Dew)*

158 : 4698 on the sidings into the canal transhipment shed, not very often glimpsed in photographs! The basin has since been developed as a marina. *(John Dew)*

159 : A canal-side view of the transhipment shed at Halesowen Basin, also known as Hawne Basin. As can be seen here, the canal to rail traffic consisted of steel tubes from The T. I. Tubeworks at Coombs Wood. This traffic ceased in June 1967. *(John Dew)*

The Earl of Dudley's Railways

The railways associated with the Earl of Dudley were the Kingswinford Railway (also known as the Shut End Railway) and the Pensnett Railway. The two lines were not physically joined until 1865, and from then on they were operated as one single system, soon afterwards simply calling themselves the Pensnett Railway.

160 : Ashwood Basin, on the Staffordshire and Worcestershire Canal. The basin was newly constructed for the Kingswinford Railway and from here the line ran to Shut End and collieries at Corbyn's Hall near Lenches Bridge. The line was built as the result of an agreement between Lord Dudley and John Foster, the proprietor of John Bradley & Co., coal and iron masters of Stourbridge, who had just begun to develop the area around Shut End. The railway opened on 2nd June 1829 and was worked by the celebrated locomotive, *"Agenoria"*. The engine was built in Stourbridge and reached the railway via this basin. (Today it lives at the York Railway Museum). The railway's main purpose was to convey coal to the canal. This picture was taken about 1930 when the basin was still in use but after the Second World War it declined and the NCB stopped sending Baggeridge coal to Stourport Power Station via the canal in October 1953.

161 : The Pensnett Railway was built to provide transport for the coal produced by Lord Dudley's pits on the parts of Pensnett Chase not reached by the Kingswinford Railway or the Stourbridge Extension Canal. One destination for such coal were the several ironworks flanking the Dudley Canal near Round Oak, including the (Old) Level Ironworks and the Nine Locks Ironworks. Eventually, in 1857, the 11th Baron Ward started the construction of Round Oak Iron Works there. The first part of the Pensnett Railway had been completed in the mid 1840s. It climbed Barrow Hill, skirted Fens Pool and reached a canal basin at the Wallows, seen in this picture. From the Wallows there was also a line that ran in one direction towards the ironworks mentioned above, and in the other direction to High Lanes (an area now buried under the new General Hospital). This view, taken between the Wars, gives some impression of the quantity of coal that reached the canal via the Pensnett Railway. *(Collection of Vic Smallshire)*

162 : The Wallows, photographed on 2nd May 1959, presents a very different picture. No coal is now transhipped at the basin, and the sidings curving away to the right now carry wagons of scrap for the hungry furnaces at Round Oak. On the left is the engine shed and administrative HQ of the Pensnett Railway, the latter now performing almost no function other than serving the Steelworks. (An identical crane still survives at the Bumble Hole Boatyard). *(P.J. Shoesmith)*

163 : If Ashwood Basin was the western extremity of the unified system that from the mid-1860s onwards was the Pensnett Railway, these three pictures illustrate its other three extremities. In the south, the Pensnett Railway reached as far as Cradley Heath where a land sale wharf was built at Forge Lane, on the opposite side of the road to the GWR's goods yard. In 1874 a physical connection was made between the PR and the GWR via a Level crossing that was just to the left of the sidings visible in this picture. Up until the Second World War it made sense to bring coal by rail to these land-sale wharves from which it could be distributed locally by horse and cart, but after the War lorries could travel further afield. The southern lines of the PR, to this yard, and to one at Old Hill, were lifted in the early 50s. *(Collection of Vic Smallshire)*

164 : The eastern extremity of the PR was its land-sale wharf at Wellington Road, Dudley, seen in this view of the sidings and weighbridge office. The latter bears the date 1864 and carries a coronet where usually the initials *"ED"* were to be found. (Queen Victoria had revived the baronetcy in 1860). The line was lifted after the Second World War but a short section of it from the Wallows to the Old Park Engineering Works remained in use until the mid sixties. *(Dudley Libraries)*

165 : The northern limit of the Pensnett Railway was Baggeridge Colliery. Many small Black Country pits served by the PR were almost worked out by the 1890s and it was decided to look for coal at a deeper level on the northern side of the Russells Hall Fault. An exploratory shaft, near Baggeridge, was sunk in 1898 and construction of a large pit along modern lines began in the early 1900s. For a time a narrow gauge line served the site from Himley Colliery No. 5. Meanwhile the GWR showed some interest in reaching the pit from the Kingswinford Branch, or more precisely, from the short Askew Bridge Branch, a spur off the former. In the event the GWR built the line up to Baggeridge Colliery, but it was part of the PR and solely operated by the PR until 1952 when the NCB took over! The line was complete by 1907 but Baggeridge Colliery did not go into full production until 1912. The Colliery closed in March 1968. This picture, taken about 1920, shows the screens and a PR loco, shunting in the sidings. *(Dudley Libraries)*

166 : Perhaps one of the best known features of the Pensnett Railway was its crossing with the GWR at Round Oak. This view, taken in the mid 1950s, shows 0-6-0ST, *"Duchess of Gloucester"* (Andrew Barclay, works number 2110 of 1941) crossing the GWR West Midland line on its way to the Wallows. The crossing became necessary when the OWWR came through Round Oak in 1852 and when sidings were added later the PR found itself crossing a number of tracks. The main line company controlled the crossing despite legends to the contrary. In 1970 it was re-aligned when the works were modernised and continued to exist until the autumn of 1983 when it was removed. *(R.O.S.W. official photograph)*

167 : Another unique feature of the Pensnett Railway was its architectural imagination applied to the design of crossing-keepers' huts. This particular hut was at the point where the railway crossed Stallings Lane on its way from the Baggeridge Colliery line to the Ashwood Basin Line. Mr. J. Walker was looking after the crossing in 1949. *(Viv Morgan)*

168 : Most interesting of all was the amazing number and variety of locomotives used by the PR in its long history. Some came to the system "second-hand", but a good many were purchased new to fulfil specific purposes. For example, this locomotive, *"Jubilee"*, an 0-6-0ST built specifically for working the line to Baggeridge came from the Andrew Barclay factory in 1935 (works number 2012). It lasted until October 1963, being cut up a few months after complete dieselisation. *(Lionel J. Lee)*

169 : As time went on the PR system became more dominated by the internal rail needs of Round Oak Steel Works (Steel production replaced iron production towards the end of the last century). The pictures on this page try to evoke the atmosphere of the line within the works. This picture, taken on 2nd May 1959 will bring back memories for many people: An Andrew Barclay 0-4-0ST stands among PR coal wagons and the tipping wagons used internally in the steel works for carrying rubbish. In the background the chimneys of the five open-hearth furnaces climb into the sky to form a landmark visible for miles. *(P.J. Shoesmith)*

170 : *"Lady Patricia"*, an Andrew Barclay 0-4-0ST (works number 1880 of 1925) standing outside the open hearth furnaces on the lines that led to the scrap dump, in 1963. *(Viv Morgan)*

171 : Between 1955 and 1963 Round Oak Steel Works took delivery of ten 0-4-0 diesel electric shunters built by the Yorkshire Engine Co. The zebra-like paintwork and the tolling bell made them very noticeable within the works and as far afield as Askew Bridge and Old Park Engineering Works. This example is seen with a pan wagon on the sidings where the pans were filled with scrap metal. *(Viv Morgan)*

At the back of Round Oak Steel Works the PR had originally continued to Saltwells, Old Hill and Cradley Heath, but as that part of the line closed the only section remaining in use was the line that crossed Level Street to reach the finishing mills at Old Level. In 1959 an Act of Parliament had to be obtained to authorise the construction of a new level crossing lower down Level Street. Both the new crossing and the old one were given lifting barriers controlled by austere, but distinctive, cabins overlooking the road.

172 : Yorkshire Engine 0-4-0 diesel No. 10 (works number 2883 of 1963 – last of the fleet) approaches the original crossing at Level Street from the finishing mills. The new cabin and barrier tended to make the observer forget that once the PR had continued from here, down a rope-worked incline, to the southern part of the system. *(Viv Morgan)*

173 : A Barclay 0-4-0ST crosses the new crossing in Level Street on 25th November 1961 as a Wallis and Stevens steam roller belonging to Mr. James rests from its work. *(John Dew)*

174 : Electric colour light signalling was installed at the crossings thus creating an intriguing juxtaposition of "ancient and modern", as the driver of an 0-4-0ST with open-backed cab confronts the new technology on 25th November 1961. *(John Dew)*

175 : The line to Baggeridge Colliery was worked by PR engines until 1952. The NCB then acquired two brand new Hunslet 0-6-0STs to work the line from the colliery to Baggeridge Junction on the Kingswinford Branch, or to Askew Bridge for collection by a PR locomotive. By 1966 the steel-works no longer needed to receive coal in this way and in the September of that year it closed the section of the PR from Askew Bridge back to the Wallows. For the previous three years a diesel had tackled the Barrow Hill incline and trundled over the embankment above Fens Pool with this traffic, but reorganisation at the Works made it redundant. On the last working, on 26th September 1966, PR 0-4-0 diesel No. 10 hands over the empty wagons to NCB 0-6-0ST No. 9 (Hunslet 3777 of 1952) at Askew Bridge. *(Collection of Viv Morgan)*

176 : NCB 0-6-0ST, No. 9, propels wagons full of coal down the "Triangle" to the point where they will be collected by a PR loco for the rest of their journey to Round Oak, on 26th October 1963. The line in the foreground led to Baggeridge Junction. *(Viv Morgan)*

177 : Again on 26th October, No. 9 is seen bringing empty wagons back from Baggeridge Junction over the bridge that crossed the disused PR line that made its way down to Shut End. *(Viv Morgan)*

The "Shaft", as the large steel works at Wednesbury was known, had a long history stretching back to the 1830s, when the manufacture of axles on the site began. In 1864 the Patent Shaft and Axletree Company was formed and three years later the neighbouring company of Lloyds Foster & Co. was absorbed so that the company no longer simply manufactured a variety of iron products but also took on blast furnaces, a Bessemer steel works, and several collieries. The internal railways systems of the three works, at Old Park, Brunswick and Monway were not fully integrated until the First World War and developed into a complex system with connections to the LNWR Darlaston Loop and South Staffordshire lines and the GWR main line.

178 : *"Monway"*, was a Hawthorn Leslie 0-4-0ST (works number 2170) built for Patent Shaft in 1889. It spent its entire life at the works and was scrapped in 1951. *(Sheila Cochrane/Black Country Society)*

179 : No. 10 was another Hawthorn Leslie 0-4-0ST (works number 2889) supplied new to the works in 1911. During the First World War, No 10 also worked at the Willingsworth Furnaces. This photograph was taken on 23rd April 1940. *(Industrial Railway Society)*

180 : The loco fleet at Patent Shaft was dieselised between 1957 and 1961 and the works itself went through a number of changes. A final modernisation plan took place in the mid 70s and a second generation of Hunslet diesels were introduced. The works closed in June 1980. Typical of the first generation of diesels at the works was *"Christopher"*, a Ruston Hornsby 0-4-0 diesel mechanical loco built in 1961 (works number 437364). It was photographed in June 1971. *(Nostalgia, Stetchford)*

181 : In 1866 Alfred Hickman took over the ailing Springvale Furnaces at Bilston and gradually built them up to be one of the biggest concerns in the Midlands. When the making of iron was eclipsed by the emergence of steel, Bilston started manufacturing the new product (an example followed by Round Oak), and steel-making carried on under the banner of Stewarts and Lloyds and then the British Steel Corporation until the end of the 1970s. Mr. Hickman established a standard gauge railway system and a connection with the LNWR Stour Vale by 1878 when the company's first loco (a Barclay) was delivered. Later the plant was also served by the GWR's West Midland Line. This view of the sidings alongside the electrified Stour Valley main line just shows Springvale Sidings Signal Box in the distance and the name of the company in red neon lighting that could be seen as far away as Dudley on a clear night!
(Wulfrun College Collection)

182 : Like all such works the plant at Bilston underwent continuous modernisation, rebuilding, rationalisation, etc. which produced a compact, yet complex, internal railway system with tortuous curves, and tight clearances, etc. A typical steelworks view is evoked by this picture of the "Landing" and the melting shop, at one time housing seven basic open-hearth furnaces. Two special Ruston Hornsby diesels, slightly smaller than usual, exclusively worked on the Landing.
(Wulfrun College Collection)

183 : This view inside the melting shop provides a glimpse of one of the small Rustons at work. Bogies, each carrying four charging boxes of scrap, were held in holding bays and carefully weighed before being despatched to the appropriate furnace. S & L stuck to open hearth furnaces while others experimented with electric arc furnaces, possibly sealing the eventual fate of the plant.
(Wulfrun College Collection)

184 : The firm of Andrew Barclay provided the majority of the locomotives at Springvale, but other locobuilders were represented, as can be seen by these examples. This 0-4-0ST was one of four at the works built by Peckett (works number 1146 of 1907), and was supplied direct to Springvale. She was still at work when this picture was taken on 14th May 1949. *(Norman Glover)*

185 : Some locomotives were acquired second-hand. In 1949 five ex Southern Railway class B4 0-6-0Ts were purchased. This particular one, eventually named *"Dorset"*, had originally been No. 99 on the SR and signs of her previous ownership are still visible. They were repainted in S & L's light green livery but were withdrawn about 1953. *(Norman Glover)*

186 : At one time narrow gauge tracks were used to carry ingots to the melting shop and 2 feet gauge engines were purchased to do this job. *"Gertrude"* came to Springvale about 1926 and was built by Andrew Barclay (works number 1578 of 1918). She was photographed here on 14th May 1949. *(Norman Glover)*

187 : In 1952 a decision was made to dieselise the railway system, while other alterations were being made to the plant. No. 12, *"Michael"*, was built by the Yorkshire Engine Company (works number 2879 of 1962) was not one of the first batch. Indeed the first such diesels to arrive were given names like *"Coronation"*, *"Elizabeth"* and *"Philip"* ! In the background, on the left, the Blast Furnace, *"Elisabeth"*, can be seen. Although built about the time of the Coronation, the name was spelt with an *"s"*, and it was named after a director's daughter. This proud furnace, that always had to be lit by a virgin, was demolished in October 1980. The picture was taken on 12th April 1979, coinciding with the casting of the last steel billet. The last three surviving YE diesels were cut up on the wasteland that had once been a steelworks in August 1983. *(Nostalgia, Stetchford)*

188 & 189 : Captions Overleaf

Previous page :

188 : Canal wharves and railway systems were important to Gas Works, in terms of bringing in supplies of coal and in terms of taking away the industry's by-products. For example, coke was sold for consumption in local furnaces. This intriguing photograph was taken at the South Staffordshire Mond Gas Co.'s works at Dudley Port. The men in the foreground are standing on a narrow boat in the basin, parallel to the main line of the BCN, that was built to serve the works. Above them *"Lance"* (built by Hawthorn Leslie, number 3155 of 1915) seems to be taking charge of a train of coke. Mond Gas was supplied to industrial customers and was not to be confused by the Town Gas, produced by a neighbouring plant, for domestic use. *(Black Country Society)*

189 : Walsall Gasworks had been a municipal operation until the Nationalisation of the gas industry in 1949. It acquired some fame in the hands of the W.M.G.B. by acquiring a brand new Sentinel locomotive in 1957 (works number 9632), photographed here on 12th April 1968. *(P.J. Shoesmith)*

This page :

190 : The works at Wolverhampton were run by the Wolverhampton Gas Co. until the formation of the W.M.G.B. The latter did not introduce any new steam locomotives to the works. *"Carbon"*, a Bagnall 0-4-0ST (works number 1673 of 1902) poses here with the LNWR Stour Valley main line's viaduct forming a backdrop. *(Industrial Railway Society)*

191 : The gas works at Swan Village was responsible for building gas holders (in at least three different designs) that became local landmarks, and employed quite a variety of locomotives. In March 1950 No. 21 was looking very smart in new W.M.G.B. livery. 21 was an 0-4-0ST built by Hudswell Clarke (works number 1734 of 1943). *(Industrial Railway Society)*

192 : In 1952 diesels arrived at Swan Village Gasworks. In the foreground, No. 1, was an 0-4-0D (built by Andrew Barclay, works number 386 of 1952). Behind the diesel is No. 21, now sporting a crest on the cabside, and in the background, with an elaborate W.M.G.B. logo on its saddle tank is No. 20. No. 20 was an 0-4-0ST built by Peckett (works number 2032 of 1942). *(Phil Lycett)*

193 : From any high vantage point on the central ridge that bisects the Black Country it has been possible to locate towns by spotting the obvious landmarks. Thus it has, up till now, been possible to locate Walsall and Tipton by spotting the giant cooling towers at Birchills and Ocker Bank respectively. Here at Birchills one of the plant's two Ruston Hornsby 0-4-0 diesels of 1949 vintage shunts one of the many sidings connected to the eastern end of the Wolverhampton-Walsall ("Midland") line, beneath the cooling towers that are now about to be demolished. *(P.J. Shoesmith)*

194 : An ex BR class 08 diesel shunter, bearing its original BR number – 3087 – but repainted in C.E.G.B. orange livery is seen shunting at Birchills on 11th April 1979. The rail link to Birchills closed altogether on 12th May 1980. *(Robert Selvey)*

195 : Just as Birchills Power Station was built close to a canal (on which coal was carried from the Short Heath Basin) the original Midland Electricity Corporation plant built at Ocker Hill in 1900 was also built alongside the canal. In this picture, taken June 1973, a Ruston Hornsby 0-4-0 diesel, (works number 245036 of 1947) is shunting rail-borne coal traffic at the coal handling plant for the newer power station built on the other side of the canal. Coal wagons reached these sidings from the Princes End Branch and a short line still serves the latest (oil-fired) power station on this site. See picture *(Nostalgia, Stetchford)*

196 : One or two industrial lines were self-contained, but usually they connected with the main line railway system, or a branch of that system. This locomotive, *"Emily"*, an 0-4-0ST built by Andrew Barclay (works number 847 of 1899), was purchased by B. Gibbons for their new line connecting their firebrick works at Lower Gornal with the Pensnett Railway just under a mile away at the foot of Barrow Hill. *(Collection of Viv Morgan)*

197 : Messrs. Gibbons introduced a second Andrew Barclay 0-4-0ST to the Dibdale Works in 1920 (works number 1653 of 1920). It bore the legend, *"Gibbons, 1920"*, on the side tanks. The railway itself continued in use until March 1938, and all trace of it has been obliterated. *(Collection of Viv Morgan)*

198 : Another small industrial system near Dudley was that of Messrs. M. & W. Grazebrook. It connected with the GWR West Midland Line at Blowers Green and crossed the main Dudley-Netherton Road (Cinder Bank) to the company's works, in an area with a long and complicated history of mining and iron-working. This Peckett 0-4-0ST, *"Grazebrook No. 2"* (works number 1931 of 1938), came new to the system in 1938 and was still very smart when photographed on 5th March 1960, within a year or two of the line being closed. The engine is posed near the shed with Cinder Bank in the background. *(Norman Glover)*

199 : In Wolverhampton Messrs. Courtaulds' works acquired their rail connection with the Wombourn Branch in August 1927. Peckett 0-4-0ST *"Dafydd"* (works number 2087 of 1948), photographed 2nd March 1957, had a Welsh name as it was originally destined for the company's works in Flint.
(Norman Glover)

200 : Later in the same year, on 30th December 1957, *"Dafydd"*, had been joined by BR (ex L. & Y. R.) 0-4-0ST No. 51204. Courtaulds hired the "pug" from BR for a couple of months.
(G.F. Bannister)

201 : The line at Courtaulds, and the entire works, have now disappeared but another little known industrial line that does still survive in Wolverhampton is to be found at British Steel's works near Horseley Fields. It connects with BR (W & WR) at Heath Town Junction. On 12th April 1979 Yorkshire Engine Co. 0-4-0 diesel (works number 2673 of 1956) stands at the works with the electrified BR line and the flats at Heath Town in the background.
(Nostalgia, Stetchford)

202 : Among the companies still using the railway system are to be found Messrs. Albright and Wilson in Oldbury (see picture 137). In this picture, taken on 21st April 1951, their Peckett 0-4-0ST (works number 917 of 1902) seems to have wandered outside the works onto BR metals. She had come to Oldbury from a Yorkshire colliery in 1930. *(Norman Glover)*

203 : Messrs. Horseley Bridge & Thomas Piggott operated an internal railway system that joined BR (SS line) at Great Bridge. The connection was remarkable for its gradient! *"J.T. Daly"*, an 0-4-0ST built by W. Bagnall (works number 2450 of 1931) spent all its life at the works and has fortunately retired to the Foxfield Light Railway where it can still be seen. This picture was taken on 4th January 1969. *(Mike Wood)*

204 : NEI – Clark Chapman/John Thompson Ltd. inherited the works of Horseley Bridge and Thomas Piggott, between Dudley Port and Great Bridge. Even after the connection with BR was severed in the late 70s this Ruston Hornsby 0-4-0 diesel (works number 408496 of 1957) still shunted over the tight curves of the internal railway system until about 1982. *(Nostalgia, Stetchford)*

205 : Messrs. Rubery Owen established a factory at Darlaston about 1884 but it was not until 1919 that they laid a railway siding into their works, having to bring the line across the Walsall Canal to do so. *"The Prince"*, an 0-4-0ST built by Andrew Barclay was their first locomotive. It had originally been built for Alfred Hickman (Springvale Furnaces) (works number 287 of 1882) but was completely rebuilt in 1942 (second works number 8212) and it is the rebuilt form that is photographed here on 3rd March 1956. *(Norman Glover)*

206 : To redress the emphasis in these pages on standard gauge locomotives and systems it is essential to include *"Portobello"*, a 3 feet 2½ inches gauge 0-4-0T thought to be built by John Smith of the Village Foundry, Coven, for the New British Iron Co. Their line, serving their own works at Corngreaves, and collieries in the Old Hill/Cradley Heath area, was quite extensive. Both the company and railway had a complex history and it is not certain when, or where, this picture was taken. *(Collection of the Black Country Society)*

207 : One small industrial line that still survives is to be found in Tipton. The South Staffordshire Wagon Company's wagon-repair works was originally connected to the GWR West Midland Line near Princes End and Coseley. Since 1968 it has been connected to the electrified Stour Valley main line and has used its own locomotives to work the sidings. On 13th January 1981, a Ruston 0-4-0 diesel (probably works number 5128843 of 1966) is seen at the "back" of the yard, near Princes End. *(Robert Selvey)*

NATIONAL COAL BOARD
NATIONAL COAL BOARD

The colliery railway that served the pits at Holly Bank and Hilton Main cannot really be regarded as part of the Black Country. Geologically it belongs to the Cannock Chase Coalfield but geographically it was remote from the rest of that Coalfield, and I have decided to "adopt" it as a finale to this book as I feel it has enough connections with the Black Country to make it worth including. If you drive from Essington, one time the home of the miners at Holly Bank, towards Wolverhampton the ridge that bisects the Black Country forms a very close and visible horizon. Another factor that unites this line with the area under consideration in this book is the course of the railway as it made its way westwards to Hilton Main. The track virtually follows the present northern boundary of our West Midlands County!

Opposite page :

208 : A line in the service of industry, and a railway displaying a degree of eccentricity: it must be a Black Country Byway! These two views of the level crossing at Bursnip Road capture the essence of the railway that served Holly Bank. About eighty years ago 0-6-0ST *"Holly Bank No. 2"* is seen leaving the colliery, heading north across Bursnip Road. The engine was built by Hudswell Clarke (works number 568 of 1900). *(Jack Haddock/Jim Evans)*

209 : About 1964 NCB No. 7, a Yorkshire Engine Co. 0-6-0 (works number 2749 of 1959), also crosses Bursnip Road by the crossing keeper's cabin/signal box perched on the end of the building that had once been the wages office and "truck shop" of the Holly Bank Colliery Co. The building has just lasted into the 80s but has probably deteriorated beyond possible preservation. *(P.J. Shoesmith)*

Holly Bank Colliery, near Essington, stopped working coal about 1927, but by then the owners had opened a new shaft at Hilton Main, near Featherstone. Work on the latter had started as early as 1919 and the Hilton Main workings had been reached underground from Holly Bank on 6th December 1923. Construction of the railway from Holly Bank to Hilton Main was going on at the same time and the extension opened in September 1924. The pit shaft at Holly Bank was retained as part of the drainage and ventilation system of the newer works The engine shed and sidings there now found themselves in the middle of the rail system rather than at its terminus. Coal brought down from Hilton Main could now be taken across Bursnip Road and a short distance to some exchange sidings where the LMS (later BR) locomotive would take over for the trip to Essington Wood Junction on the Walsall-Cannock Line. However the real link with the Black Country was another line that turned east and the southwards from the exchange sidings to convey coal down to a land-sale wharf at Short Heath, and a basin on the Wyrley and Essington Canal, about a mile from the centre of Willenhall.

This page :

210 : All four pictures on this page were taken on 15th June 1965. A Bagnall diesel brings a train down to Short Heath. Note that beyond the first four wagons are wagons bearing three "containers".

211 : The crane, capable of lifting and emptying the containers of coal, at work in the land-sale wharf at Short Heath. (Compare this 1965 view with the earlier views of land-sale wharves on the Pensnett Railway.)

212 : The line continued across Wesley Road via an ungated level crossing in order to reach the canal basin. Motorists must have found this rather a surprise in the mid sixties.

213 : By that time the basin was near the end of its life, as can be seen in this rather desolate view looking towards the canal. Hilton Main colliery closed in 1969 and the railway system was demolished. The canal basin was eventually "saved" by the West Midlands County Council, in association with local councils and the British Waterways Board. In the late seventies it was dredged, the towpath was reinstated and the surrounding area was landscaped. *(All 4 pictures by P.J. Shoesmith)*

Both the GWR and LMS main lines crossed the Black Country on SE/NW axis from Birmingham to Wolverhampton. Even today the ex LMS line, "the Stour Valley line" provides a fascinating panoramic view of the region. Unfortunately the recent devastation of industry has led to a feeling that the lineside must be "cleaned up" in order to attract new industry to come to the region. Other railways once provided an even better transect, such as the West Midland line and the South Staffordshire line. However for many people today a journey across the Black Country means a journey along the Wolverhampton–Birmingham "New" Road.

This highway was built in the mid twenties, following the eastern side of the Black Country ridge where the Ten Yard Seam had been removed to leave an "emptiness" that was largely filled by subsequent ribbon development. It was built by Sir Robert McAlpine & Sons and they used a number of contractors' light railways and "steam navvies" to complete the task. The road was opened by the Prince of Wales (later Edward VIII) on 2nd November 1927.

214 : McAlpine's standard gauge 0-6-0STs, built by Hudswell Clarke, can be seen on the lightly laid track at Bury Hill, Oldbury. *(Birmingham Libraries)*

215 : At Tipton, near Burnt Tree Island, narrow gauge trains removed the spoil on this section of the road.

216 : The motorist travelling the length of the New Road passes under three railway bridges, all built for the opening of the road. On the GWR bridge near the Black Country Museum the track has been lifted that once carried the West Midland line from Dudley to Wolverhampton. On the GWR bridge near Oldbury the motorist can often glimpse the frequent trains on the Stourbridge Extension Line. Only the LMS bridge near Burnt Tree Island is an enigma: open for traffic but no-one ever seems to see a train! At present the few trains that cross the bridge do so stealthily at dawn or dusk. For example class 56 Co-Co, 56087, sneaks back to Bescot after bringing the Freightliner train to Dudley at 7.30 a.m. on 28th August 1984.

Other Black Country 'references' in this picture include, advertising for the local brew, advertising for Don Everall who began his transport-orientated career as a taxi driver outside Wolverhampton station, and the wall, on the right, of Babcock Power – the last company in Great Britain to build a Victorian GWR engine: a replica of Dean Single 3041, "*Achilles*". *(Ned Williams)*